T0247618

THE
POWER
OF
CLOSURE

THE POWER OF CLOSURE

Why We Want It, How to Get It, and When to Walk Away

Gary McClain, PhD

A TARCHERPERIGEE BOOK

tarcherperigee

an imprint of Penguin Random House LLC
penguinrandomhouse.com

Copyright © 2024 Gary McClain

Penguin Random House supports copyright. Copyright fuels creativity, encourages diverse voices, promotes free speech, and creates a vibrant culture. Thank you for buying an authorized edition of this book and for complying with copyright laws by not reproducing, scanning, or distributing any part of it in any form without permission. You are supporting writers and allowing Penguin Random House to continue to publish books for every reader. TarcherPerigee with tp colophon is a registered trademark of Penguin Random House LLC.

Most TarcherPerigee books are available at special quantity discounts for bulk purchase for sales promotions, premiums, fund-raising, and educational needs. Special books or book excerpts also can be created to fit specific needs. For details, write: SpecialMarkets@penguinrandomhouse.com.

Library of Congress Cataloging-in-Publication Data

Names: McClain, Gary R., author.
Title: The power of closure: why we want it, how to get it,
and when to walk away / Gary McClain, PhD.
Description: 1 edition. | New York: TarcherPerigee,
Penguin Random House LLC, [2024] | Includes index.
Identifiers: LCCN 2023045930 (print) | LCCN 2023045931 (ebook) |
ISBN 9780593545355 (hardcover) | ISBN 9780593545379 (epub)
Subjects: LCSH: Memory. | Recognition (Psychology) | Loss (Psychology)
Classification: LCC BF371 .M378 2024 (print) | LCC BF371 (ebook) |
DDC 153.1/2—dc23/eng/20240108
LC record available at https://lccn.loc.gov/2023045930
LC ebook record available at https://lccn.loc.gov/2023045931

Printed in the United States of America
1st Printing

Book design by Stephanie Kowalsky

To anyone who has ever tried to find closure with another human: those who were successful, those who were not, and those who accepted when it was time to walk away. In the pages of this book, it is my hope to provide you with guidance, encouragement, and some comfort for the road ahead.

CONTENTS

THE
POWER
OF
CLOSURE

Introduction

I f I could just get some closure . . ."
    Have you heard someone say these words lately? Or maybe
even said them yourself? I suspect so. That's probably why you
picked up this book.

Well, me too. In my more than twenty years as a mental health
professional, this is one of the sentences I've heard most often.
Whether my clients are in therapy to deal with grief, the loss of a
job, the end of a relationship, family dysfunction, a devastating
medical diagnosis, or a whole host of other problems, they often
raise the same question: How do I find closure?

When you think of closure, what comes to mind? Perhaps it's
the end of a romantic relationship. After a breakup, it's only hu-
man to want to have a few final words, to express how you feel, to
try to understand what happened, to end things "once and for all"
(or to see if the relationship still has a chance). Or perhaps it's the
death of a loved one. When someone dies, no matter how healthy
or unhealthy your relationship with them was, there will almost
certainly be things left unsaid that can now never be expressed, or
other loose ends that can never be tied up. Of course we wish we
could find closure, even if—*especially* if—it's impossible.

Here is the basic truth about closure, as I have experienced it in my own life and in the lives of my clients: Sometimes we find the closure we want. Sometimes we have to walk away. Walking away from the closure you thought you needed and realize you can't have can be an act of empowerment! That's the power of closure: it makes an impact on you when you find it *and* when you don't.

That is why I wrote this book. After many accumulated years of conversations around this topic, I realized it's something nearly everyone becomes fixated on at some point yet few people truly understand. In these pages, I'll explain what closure really is, why we want it, how to get it, and what to do when we can't get it. (Spoiler alert: More often than not, we don't get it.)

I suspect you didn't pick up my book because you were looking for an easy summer read. You probably chose it because you're struggling to achieve closure somewhere in your life. If so, I have a lot of compassion for you, and I am deeply honored that you picked up my book. It is my desire, my goal, that after reading the chapters ahead, you'll come away with something of personal value: a thought, an example, some insight that you can apply to your own life and, as a result, confidently seek the closure you need— or, on the other hand, recognize that it's time to walk away. Life doesn't always give us what we want, but if we're open to learning the lesson, life frequently gives us what we need.

My conversations around closure have been both heartwarming and heartbreaking, accompanied by emotions like sadness, frustration, anger, and fear, but also relief, happiness, sheer joy, and hope. I hope that in the pages ahead, you will find a combination of practical advice and support that will help you to navigate closure—or the lack thereof—in your own life. Knowing that you might benefit from reading my words is the realization of a life-long dream. Maybe someday you'll let me know. Maybe it will give me closure of my own.

Part I
Closure Defined

Chapter 1

What Closure Is

When you work in the mental health field, like I do, you find yourself having certain conversations over and over. Each of my therapy clients is an individual with their own life experiences, perspectives, and goals, but certain topics have a way of emerging and reemerging. One of these topics is closure. And while each of my clients is unique, sometimes the same words come out of their mouths.

"If I could just get some closure . . ."

"He really owes me closure on this."

"Why is she running away from giving me closure?"

And all too often: "I demand closure!"

But what *is* closure, and why do we always seem to want it so badly? Despite how often we talk about it, it can be surprisingly hard to define.

In a literal sense, the word *closure* indicates something drawing to a close, such as the end of a romantic relationship, the end of a professional relationship, or most heartbreaking of all, the end of a life. But closure is more complex than that. In fact, sometimes closure is not about an end at all, but rather about bringing some kind of a resolution to an issue that seems to come up all the time.

How do you know if you're suffering from lack of closure? Here are some of the signs. You might find yourself . . .

- Reaching out to someone to request a conversation about what happened between the two of you.
- Rehearsing what you want to say to someone to make them understand how you're feeling. (And having lots of uncomfortable feelings as you rehearse how you think they'll respond—or how you *want* them to respond.)
- Holding a vision of what your relationship with someone will look like after you have the "big talk."
- Fantasizing about how someone might feel when you "get back" at them for what they did to you.

Or you might find yourself wanting to . . .

- Return to where you think the relationship needs to be, with each of you giving and receiving in an equitable manner.
- Finally get what you deserve that the other person has been consciously or unconsciously withholding.
- Have a burden of guilt lifted when the other person finally forgives you and lets you off the hook for something you did to them—or conversely, you might want them to ask you for your forgiveness (which you may or may not grant).
- Receive acknowledgment and respect for what you contribute.

If any of the statements on these lists struck a chord with you, then you may be feeling the need for closure.

Examples of Wanting Closure

Sometimes the best way to define something is to give examples, so here are a few composite examples of clients in my practice who talked with me about their own reasons for wanting closure.

Allie and her boyfriend broke up after being together for over two years. Things had been getting rocky between them for the last couple of months—she's still not sure why. The breakup itself happened suddenly, during an argument that led to them both deciding to walk away from the relationship. Allie and her now ex have texted a few times since that night, just checking on each other. She has asked him to get together and talk about what happened, but he refuses to do so. "I have to have some kind of closure," she says. "Why won't he give that to me?" Allie feels emotional pain and the desire for forgiveness, plus some real anger . . .

Tommy was recently laid off from his job of five years. He and his boss didn't always see eye to eye, and his boss jumped on him more than once when he wasn't happy with Tommy's performance. But overall, Tommy thought they were getting along fine. Then Tommy was called into HR and given his layoff notice. His boss wasn't in the office that day, so Tommy packed up his belongings and left. He has repeatedly emailed his boss to ask if they can talk about what happened, and his boss hasn't responded. "He at least owes me some answers as to what happened with my job," Tommy says. "Can't I get some closure?" Tommy feels frustration, fear of the future, and a sense of gross unfairness . . .

Amanda is living with a chronic condition and has been working with the same physician for years. When Amanda says she loves her doctor, she means it. They have been through some rough times together. Amanda has especially appreciated being able to open up to her doctor and tell her what's on her mind. Last week, Amanda received a letter informing her that her physician had left the practice and providing her with the name of the doctor her case has been transferred to. Amanda is devastated. "I'm embarrassed to admit this," she tells me, "but I thought she would say goodbye and tell me how to stay in touch. It wouldn't have made her leaving any less sad, but at least I would have had closure." Amanda feels sadness and disappointment, along with the potential problems of adjusting to a new provider . . .

I have many other stories to tell about closure, some from the lives of my clients and some from my own life. Some of these stories end well, some don't, but all illustrate our fundamental need for closure.

Big life events—breakups, job loss, death—are most likely to press that psychological button that seeks closure. But I also want to note that our innate need for closure is so strong that it comes up in every part of our lives, even in relatively insignificant situations.

Here are a few examples.

You're in a rush, and you dive into a drugstore to pick up a prescription. You wait your turn, pay for your purchase, and dash out the door. Suddenly you realize that you didn't take the time to respond to the pharmacy tech who smiled and thanked you. You worry you came off as rude. You think about how the next time you're in that particular pharmacy, you hope you encounter the same pharmacy tech so you can be extra polite. You even consider going back in to apologize for being in such a rush. What you're looking for is closure.

Or say you're in a meeting with a group of coworkers, discussing a project. As you describe an issue you're trying to solve, another coworker cuts you off midsentence and offers a solution identical to the one you were just outlining. You don't say anything, because in the grand scheme of things it's not a huge deal, but you're left with a feeling of being wronged. Should you have confronted this person in the meeting? Talked to them later? Gone to your boss? What you do know is that you just can't let go of this without somehow closing the loop. All those questions mean you want closure.

Toward a Definition of *Closure*

As I've said, it's hard to pin down a precise definition of *closure*, but I'll do my best. As I see it, closure is an emotional state defined by a sense of finality and clarity. It means you feel little to no lingering ambiguity about a situation. Your questions have largely been answered, even if you don't necessarily like all the answers. When you *don't* have closure about a situation, you think about it often, even obsessively, trying to figure out why things happened the way they did or imagining how things might have gone if you had acted differently. When you *do* have closure, you may or may not be happy with how a situation turned out, but you understand it relatively well, and you no longer feel compelled to spend a huge amount of time and mental energy on it; you can move on and focus on other things.

The most satisfying and sought-after forms of closure often involve honest communication between people and peaceful resolution of conflict, resulting in an outcome you *are* overall happy with. But that's not the only form of closure that exists. Closure can be sad or painful. It can leave you regretting—but hopefully understanding—the actions of the other person (or your own actions). You may not always like the answers to your questions, but if they are answered satisfactorily and you feel able to put the past behind you, congratulations, that's closure.

Let's say someone you had been dating for a couple of years recently broke up with you. And let's say you were totally shocked, not having seen this coming. Things seemed fine to you, when all of a sudden: bam! You'd probably want some kind of closure, right?

Here's one way that might happen: You and your ex meet up. You talk about what each of you brought to the relationship, in ways that both contributed to and detracted from your success as a couple. You both feel like you learn a lot about yourselves from this discussion—what you do well in relationships and what you need to work on, as well as what you should be seeking in a future partner. After you talk, you hug and walk away, maybe tearful, maybe smiling, maybe feeling some regret that things didn't go better in the relationship, but now with clarity on why they didn't.

I think of this as a prime example of the closure we would all like to experience when a relationship ends. Hollywood couldn't have scripted it any better. When I have a client in this situation and we're discussing closure, this kind of scenario is what they're most hoping for. And while it may not be super common, it does happen—or at least some version of it does.

But here is an alternate scenario: Your ex arrives at your meeting place visibly agitated. Before you can speak, they launch into a verbal attack, blaming you for everything that went wrong in your relationship and telling you what an awful person they think you are. You can't get a word in edgewise. Finally, you get up from the table and walk away, leaving your ex sitting alone with their anger.

You probably feel sad, angry, and frustrated at not having a chance to tell your own side of the story, but maybe this unpleasant experience did answer some questions for you. If you were wondering whether the relationship had another chance, you can now be sure that it doesn't. Or maybe you come to the realization that your ex was not a reasonable or kind person, and that you're better off without them. These may not be the Hollywood endings we all want, but if they bring you to a place of understanding and let you move on with your life, they can be their own form of closure.

Closure comes in many different forms, and one of the keys to gaining closure, as I will discuss in future chapters, is opening your mind to the possibility that not getting closure in the form that you expected doesn't necessarily mean you don't have it. The closure we want, need, or think we deserve doesn't always happen the way we hoped, but even less-than-ideal closure can resolve our ambiguities and leave us feeling liberated.

The Human Need for Closure

What's closure got to do with it? For my clients, the answer to this question is often: Everything! Or at least their mental health, their happiness, and their self-esteem, to name just a few of the things they believe are at stake for them. Our desire for closure comes from a need to express our feelings, to fully understand why an event occurred, to find a way forward. We may seek closure for other reasons as well: to forgive or be forgiven, to clarify things after a misunderstanding, to heal our own feelings.

Why is our need for closure so strong? Human beings are hardwired to avoid uncertainty. We fight it. We deny it. We run from it. And as a result, we suffer. We have a natural discomfort with loose ends, unspoken words, unshared feelings, obligations we fear we haven't fulfilled. Humans want to *know*. We don't like to be left hanging, not knowing why an event occurred, not knowing why another person chose to behave as they did. And depending on our own level of defensiveness, we also want to know what we ourselves may have done to contribute to the situation.

This very human desire to know can lead us to find the understanding we seek. But it can also lead to obsession, causing us to place ourselves in disempowering situations that lead nowhere. And in the absence of real information, our minds are all too willing to step in and create stories for us that can lead to more pain and suffering.

When we imagine getting closure, it seems so simple. Two adults sit down and work things out. Describe their individual perspectives. Listen and understand. Come to an agreement of some kind in terms of how to move on, with or without each other. But as we know, humans are pretty complicated. Sorting out emotions and egos is not easy work, as any therapist will tell you. It requires being able to express how you feel, to give words to thoughts and feelings. It requires being able to listen without being defensive. It requires some give-and-take. In my experience, when you seek closure from another person, you're asking them to be open, to be vulnerable, to be willing to step up to the plate and have an honest discussion with you. That can be a lot to ask for when you and the other person are both trapped in your own humanity, with all its gifts, flaws, and contradictions.

Closing Thought:
My Own Story about Closure

My mom always used to say, "If I had a nickel every time somebody said . . ." I often feel that way about the word *closure*. As a therapist, I'm sure I'm not unique in that regard. But I have to say that closure has been a recurring theme in my own life, and I often wonder if I attract clients who are also trying to figure out how to deal with it. As I began writing this book, my heart was heavy with my most recent struggle with closure. Here is my story (or one of them, at least).

My close friend David owns property in the country where he grew up, and on a friend's recommendation, he hired a friendly and motivated young man named Victor to help with maintenance work. Both David and I thought Victor had a lot of potential. David decided to mentor him and began providing regular financial support for basic expenses, tuition for education, and other assistance to him and his family. I also befriended Victor, and I helped out occasionally with a bit of money, as well as a new computer.

But after a couple of years, David made some greatly disappointing discoveries. He learned that Victor had not been using the money he'd accepted in the manner he said he was, and that he had invented stories to make sure the financial support continued. David had given Victor a significant amount of money and was now injured both emotionally and financially. It was painful for me to see how deeply betrayed he felt.

After everything fell apart and David ended his relationship with Victor, I was visiting this country again. Victor, whom I hadn't spoken with since this all happened, asked if we could have dinner together. I decided to go because, yes, I wanted some kind of closure. Unfortunately, I didn't get it. Throughout the meal, Victor told me about things going on in his life that I knew were not at all the truth. I felt somewhat betrayed, but more than that, I was worried about him, the decisions he was making, and where his life was going.

Victor continued to text me after I returned to the US, and I hesitated to respond because I felt like I needed to take David's side. But David left it up to me, so after a few days I briefly responded with a few words: *I hope you are okay.* Soon after this, Victor blocked me.

After I lost contact with Victor, my desire for closure gradually grew, and in my mind, I conjured up a very specific image of how I thought it should happen. I wanted Victor to own up to his lies and apologize to me. I wanted to accept his apology. I told myself that this would be a growth opportunity for him, but yes, I knew my own ego was also involved. (Our egos are always involved.) I wanted to be in touch with him—and to help him as needed, if I could do that in a way that would not leave my friend David feeling further betrayed.

Two years passed. During that time, I had no idea what Victor was doing with his life, how he was living, if he was okay or not.

One day, David called me at work. I could hear that he was crying as he spoke. He told me that Victor had died of cancer, which we'd had no idea he had. I thought back to the frequent illnesses that he seemed to have, the help that he periodically needed in paying hospital bills. I thought about the last time I saw him and how emaciated he'd felt when I hugged him goodbye. Answers to previously unanswered questions clicked into place. I realized that he had probably been sick the whole time we had known him but had never told us of his illness. What demons had this young man been walking with, including possibly the specter of his own death? Why didn't he tell us? Why, why, why? Things could have gone so differently. We could have helped in the ways he and his family needed the most. I demanded answers. My rational mind told me getting answers was not going to be possible, but I demanded them anyway!

For a few days, I found myself sitting in my office and crying between clients. I told everyone that the red eyes were the result of allergies. And as I sat with my tears, I again thought about closure. I fantasized about flying with David to his country, bringing food to Victor and his family, making sure he was receiving good care. I envisioned sitting by Victor's bed, telling him that he was appreciated and forgiven and loved, asking his forgiveness for not trying harder to stay in touch. Most of all, I wanted to hug him.

I wanted closure. I wanted a second chance to get this closure. Really bang-up, fantastic closure that would leave us all feeling like the end of a Hallmark movie.

Yet again, closure eluded me.

I felt sadness for myself and for my friend David and for this young man Victor. I felt sadness for all the other times in my life when I've needed closure that I couldn't get. I felt sadness for my clients who are struggling to live their lives without the closure they need to move on. I was reminded of the many, many times when clients sat on my couch and talked about their own lack of closure. Breakups. Divorces. Layoffs. Relocations. Medical diagnoses. Deaths. Clients who wept into their hands as they described wanting to know! Needing to know! Deserving to know! And yet . . . not knowing.

It is only human to want closure. Seeking closure can lead to resolution and growth, or it can lead to frustration and more pain. But even the pain of not finding closure can lead to personal growth in the end. Seeking closure has been a painful but also rewarding process in my own life and in the lives of my clients. For you too? I invite you to join me on the closure journey.

Chapter 2

What Closure Is Not

O ne way to better understand what closure *is*, is to look at what it *is not*. If closure is a state of finality, clarity, and peace, then the opposite of closure might be defined as something like disturbance, distraction, or unhealthy, obsessive rumination. But once again, it's more complicated than that, because when we seek closure, we generally have an outcome in mind. And whether the actual outcome is ultimately positive or negative, it's often very different from what we expected.

So for this chapter, let's focus on three things that are commonly mistaken for closure but which are not, in fact, closure: Closure is not revenge. Closure is not control. And, though they're related, closure is not acceptance.

Closure Is Not Revenge

When was the last time the idea of getting revenge crossed your mind? Last month? Last week? About an hour ago? If you answered yes to any of these questions, let me assure you that you are normal. Actually, if you said you'd never felt the urge for revenge, I would be surprised. When we feel we have been wronged or intentionally harmed in some way, we want to "get back at" the person responsible (or the person we perceive as being responsible), in a way that causes them to also feel pain.

That's human nature. But it's not closure.

A question to ask yourself if you're contemplating finding closure: Do I want to gain healthy closure with this person, or do I just want to make them hurt the same way I hurt? Revenge is frequently a motivator for closure at some level. It may not be all-out, in-your-face revenge that leaves the other person a whimpering pile of emotions. But the need for just a drop or two of revenge—making someone feel sad or guilty, for example—may find its way into your plans for closure.

Take James and Anna. They had what they thought was a pretty amazing relationship. They were both in their early thirties, settled in their careers, and attractive, with many friends. Calling them a perfect couple didn't seem like an overstatement. Until it was.

After they'd been living together for a few years, Anna's company, a startup, finally reached critical mass and became successful. Anna had a leadership role in the company, so the demands on her increased exponentially, as did her work hours. This was Anna's opportunity to make a big splash in her field, and she seized it. She left their apartment early each morning and returned late at night. Once a week or so, she ended up catching a few hours of sleep on the couch in her office and continued working through the next day and evening.

Anna's long hours at work included lengthy meetings with the CEO of the company, Jonathan. James had met him a few times at company events, and while Jonathan seemed like an affable guy, James decided he didn't trust him once Anna's hours away from home increased. He observed Jonathan and Anna together at a party, and he didn't appreciate the way Jonathan put his hand on Anna's shoulder while they talked.

One evening, as James sat alone at home watching TV, ruminating about Anna's long work hours and how he felt left behind, he decided to wait up for Anna. When she arrived, around midnight, James was primed. He told her he didn't trust Jonathan and he didn't like the extended hours she was working. He gave her an ultimatum: leave the job or leave the relationship.

Anna was shocked that James would accuse her of being unfaithful. She was hurt and angry that he would attempt to control her life and rob her of a great career opportunity. She told him how she felt. She also told him that she didn't see how they could go on as a couple if he distrusted her so much. James angrily agreed that if she couldn't see his side of things, then she needed to leave. She packed a bag and moved into a hotel that night. A few days later, she came to the apartment while James was at work and removed the rest of her belongings.

James was all over the place emotionally after what he was finally able to admit to himself was their breakup. He'd misjudged how Anna would react. He had thought that she would apologize for abandoning him. He'd assumed she would want to sit down and work things out. And yes, he'd predicted that she valued their relationship more than her job and might even quit the next day. But that wasn't how things went.

After she moved out, he and Anna had only brief conversations, mainly to tie up loose ends about owed money and forwarding addresses. He texted her a few times and received only short responses: *Yes, I am okay. Hope you are too.* He felt like he deserved some closure after the time they'd spent together, the home they'd built, the plans they'd made. So he asked if they could get together. He told her he thought it was important to talk about what had happened. He wanted her to know how he was feeling now that he was less overwhelmed by emotions. It would be good for both of them to have closure, he said.

James gave this conversation a lot of thought. In fact, he started rehearsing it. He would speak from the heart, he told himself. He and Anna had never really talked things through. That's what his friends and family recommended: Talk things out. Come to an understanding. Hug and wish each other great success.

But in James's mind, "talking things out" was about teaching Anna a lesson. He decided he would tell Anna how neglectful she was of their relationship, and how he would never believe she and Jonathan weren't having an affair. He would also inform her that the sex was never that good and that he never felt as happy as he needed to feel in their relationship. Didn't he deserve to have her know this? he asked himself. Of course. And wouldn't it be beneficial for her to know? Of course. And shouldn't Anna feel some of the hurt that he felt? Of course. That might finally give him the closure he needed.

Revenge is sweet . . . until it isn't. I've been in this business for a long time, and I can say with confidence that I have never heard anyone who took revenge on another person say that they were satisfied afterward. In the moment, it might work masterfully: the other person is damaged, humiliated, devastated. But afterward, do you feel peaceful and clear? More likely, you feel ashamed, embarrassed, and empty. Revenge is a temporary victory that all too often ends up feeling like a defeat. When revenge is masquerading as closure, it only leads to the need for more closure, to fix the damage done to yourself and the other person, as well as the need to ask for forgiveness.

That's what happened to James. When he delivered his speech, the satisfaction he received was only temporary. It lasted until Anna began to cry. Seeing how he hurt someone who had meant so much to him left James longing for more closure. Now he wanted to apologize, to let Anna know that he didn't really feel that way about her. Not at all. He wanted to tell her that he was just angry and wanted to get back at her for how she had disappointed him.

But after that, Anna cut off all communication with him. James's need for closure remained just as intense as it had been leading up to that conversation, and he's going to have to sit with it for a heck of a long time.

If you're not sure whether you're looking for closure or revenge, take a step back, identify your emotions, and think about your reasons for wanting closure, as well as the potential consequences. Human motivation is seldom 100 percent pure, but are you trying to tie up loose ends and create mutual understanding, or are you hoping to cause pain? The first is closure. The second is not. Revenge-fueled closure is a trip to nowhere.

Closure Is Not Control

I can't tell you how often someone asks me how they can make someone do something. "How do I make him give me credit for being a smart and competent person?" "How do I make her acknowledge all the things I do for her?" "How do I make this person understand how much I care about them?" "How can I make this person explain to me why they behaved that way?" And they launch into a story about trying to change someone's thoughts, feelings, or behavior.

As much as we might like to deny it, the simple truth is that we can't control how other people think, feel, or behave. We just can't. Accepting that fact can save us a whole lot of heartache, especially when it comes to closure.

Most of the time when I talk with a client about closure, they have a very clear picture of what they want it to look like. Some visions are more realistic than others. They may be based on what the client thinks the other person is capable of, what they think would be best for themselves and for the other person, or what they feel they deserve. (Especially what they feel they deserve.) But the bottom line is that they have in mind a specific image of the closure they want to achieve.

I often ask these clients to imagine various outcomes they might experience. I say to them, "Given what you know about the person you're seeking closure from, what are the possible ways they might respond to your request?" This question is often met with some resistance. After all, it's hard to let go of what you feel is your right to closure or what you feel is the appropriate response from the other person. Of course it is. As we know, human beings have an aversion to anything left hanging. Our minds have a way of presenting us with all kinds of scenarios to make sense of things we don't understand. With closure, it's only natural to latch on to the one that most closely resembles what would help us feel vindicated, missed, or just overall less burdened. But subconsciously we think things should happen the way we want them to.

Sometimes it works out that way. But often it doesn't. The closure we achieve may look nothing like the closure we envisioned, for better or for worse. We may not achieve closure at all.

If you have experienced the death of an acquaintance, friend, or family member, I suspect you have felt, at some level, a lack of closure. This could be a wistfulness about a few words you wish you had shared with this person, something you would have liked them to know. Or you may be engulfed in grief, begging the universe for one last moment with this person to express what you wish you had expressed when you thought you had time.

Imagine being a young adult and losing one of your best friends in a car accident. While dealing with the intense and painful feelings of loss, you might contact your friend's family and ask to visit them to express your condolences and share memories of your friendship with their child. This would certainly be an appropriate gesture under these circumstances. You might show them pictures of their child and your friend group, and they might share stories of your friend as a young child. You would laugh together, cry together. You would go home that day acutely aware of your grief, but also with a feeling of closure in having shared this time with your friend's parents, knowing you had celebrated your friend's life and supported one another in your mutual pain.

And if it happens that way, then great. But none of that is under your control. Grief is complicated. If you have experienced the death of a loved one, you know that people experiencing grief don't always act in a predictable, or even rational, manner. Because of that, we have to give ourselves space to cope with our feelings, and we have to give others space. It is entirely possible in this scenario that, after reaching out to the parents, you don't get a warm or welcoming response. Instead, you receive a brief note thanking you and asking you to respect the family's desire for privacy, along with a suggestion of a charity you might donate to in your friend's memory.

In this version of the story, you don't receive the closure you wanted—but that doesn't mean you won't receive it at all. You might work toward closure by reminiscing with your friend group, attending your friend's funeral, engaging in practices like prayer or meditation if you're a spiritual person, or any number of other ways. But if the only scenario you're open to is the one where everything goes the way you want it to, you're probably going to be waiting a long time for closure.

So how do you make someone give you closure? You don't, actually. Humans are unpredictable and uncontrollable. You're only half of the equation (or less than half, if multiple people are involved). It's what keeps life interesting, and often frustrating. That doesn't mean your need for closure isn't valid, or that seeking closure isn't worthwhile. But if you do find closure, it won't be because you found a way to control the situation or make someone do what you wanted them to do. That's the bad news and the good news about closure.

Closure Is Not (Quite) Acceptance

Because you have limited control in any given situation, the truth is that you may *never* receive closure. You might never get the answers you want or have the opportunity to speak your piece. Ambiguity and questions will continue to linger. Yet you can still eventually come to terms with reality, accept things for what they are, and move forward with your life.

Let's say you suddenly lost your job. You didn't see it coming. Your company reorganized, and you found yourself without a role in your department. And to make it even more painful, let's imagine you were escorted out of the building an hour after receiving the news, having been provided with cardboard boxes for your belongings and a big bulky envelope from HR. Clients of mine who have been in this situation describe their initial reaction as shock, followed by intense sadness and anger. Most likely you feel you should have received a warning from your boss. You probably would want to know why your role was suddenly viewed as unnecessary and if you had done something to place yourself in this position.

If you came into my office and told me you wanted to seek closure, I would ask you to talk with me about your expectations. Here's the ideal scenario that clients often describe: You meet your former boss for coffee. You have a friendly discussion about all your contributions. Your boss reminds you of how talented you are, and how infinitely employable. Maybe they even offer to connect you with people in their professional network who might be able to help you land your next position. The conversation ends with a few tears as your boss expresses regret at the company's decision and asks forgiveness for not being able to advocate for you like they wanted to.

But in reality, that's probably not how it will happen. Instead, it's likely that when you reach out, your boss will just read from a script prepared by HR, stating that your job loss was a business decision and not personal, and reminding you of the phone number you can call if you have questions about your severance package. Or you might send an email to your boss and receive no response at all—or even worse, a single sentence requesting that you not contact them again.

As we've discussed, you don't control other people, and you can't force your boss or anyone else at your former company to hear your side of the story or answer your questions about why and how this happened. Although a job loss can leave you with a desire for closure that can feel like an obsession, closure in the scenario described above is probably impossible.

Does that mean you'll be bitterly ruminating on it your whole life? Maybe. But maybe you'll find a new job you like, develop good relationships with new coworkers, and continue advancing your career. You may never get satisfactory answers about why you were laid off or why your boss treated you the way they did, but eventually you can come to accept that as one of life's mysteries and spend your time and energy on living your life the way you want to.

That's not exactly closure, but it is acceptance, and it's the healthiest thing to strive for when closure isn't in the cards.

Closing Thought: A Working Definition of *Closure*

So now we have a working definition of *closure*. It's a sense of clarity and peace in which we feel loose ends have been tied up. We have an innate desire for it, but our motivations and the ways we try to get it can be healthy or unhealthy, because we are all humans with our own flaws and imperfections. In the best-case scenario, closure involves people honestly communicating and reaching a place of mutual understanding and forgiveness. In the worst-case scenario, we don't get it at all—but we can find other ways to gain peace and move on.

Now let's begin the work of understanding and seeking closure.

Part II
Why We Want Closure

Chapter 3

We're Hurting

Now that we've established a good understanding of what closure is and is not, let's delve into the reasons we typically seek closure. The chapters in this section will offer deep dives into the complicated and all-too-human reasons we want closure—presumably some of the very reasons you picked up this book. We'll start with the simplest one: we want closure because we're just plain hurting.

What can take away intense emotional pain? I sat with that question as I wrote this chapter. I ask it again and again when I meet with clients who have pain that is so deep they're inconsolable. I take seriously my role in supporting them and helping to guide them through it, to get to whatever the other side of their pain will look like for them. And one of the most common questions they ask me is: "How can I get some kind of closure?"

Emotional pain can impact us so profoundly that it almost feels physical. Maybe that's where the idea of "dying from a broken heart" came from. If you believe in the body-mind-spirit connection like I do, then you could say that emotional and physical pain are indeed connected. Physicians I have spoken with about pain management have often told me that it's hard for a patient to describe physical pain in a way that lets them determine the best way to help, resulting in a trial-and-error approach to pain management. I actually think mental health professionals might have an easier time understanding the depth of pain their clients are experiencing. Phrases I have heard include: "It's so bad I can't get through the day." "I feel like I'm going to collapse under the weight." "I'm in so much pain I just want to crawl into a hole and wait until it finally stops." Hearing phrases like these from my clients sets off an alarm with me. I know this is a patient suffering deeply.

Deep pain can interfere with your relationships, causing you to isolate, to blow up out of anger, or to feel especially needy. At its most extreme, it can feel like it's taken over your whole life. You've lost your power to feel optimistic, joyful, capable. Your life has become all about emotional pain.

Have you ever had pain this deep? I suspect you have. I sure have. And I suspect somewhere along the way, you also felt that finding some kind of closure was the only way you could go forward. Can closure make this pain go away? Something has to! Right?

WHEN TO SEE A PROFESSIONAL

If your emotional pain is unrelenting, then what you may need the most is to reach out to a mental health professional. Regardless of whether you need closure or not, unending emotional pain may be a sign of something deeper, such as depression or another form of mental illness. This is nothing to be ashamed of. Emotional pain, and any associated mental illness, is treatable. The first step is to meet with a mental health professional, talk about how your pain is affecting your life, and work together on a treatment plan. Working with a mental health professional can also help you achieve closure, but it is a process that takes one step at a time, and a treatment plan may need to come first.

The Pain of Loss

We often think of deep emotional pain in terms of a loss. This might be the loss of a loved one. The loss of a job. The loss of vibrant health due to a medical diagnosis. The loss of a relationship. The loss of a secure home due to a disaster, natural or financial.

My client Miguel lost the person he thought he would call his best friend forever. His name was Damian. They were living like many twentysomethings do, sharing an apartment, inviting friends over, introducing each other to potential dates. One weekend, Damian got in his car to drive to his parents' home for the weekend. On the way, his car was hit by a drunk driver, and he was killed instantly. To say that Miguel was emotionally destroyed by Damian's death doesn't begin to describe how he felt. He was overwhelmed by his grief.

In our conversations, Miguel talked about what a good friend Damian had been to him. He realized how much he had depended on Damian. They had fun together, but they also provided emotional support and stability to each other, in the way that friends who become family members do. Miguel asked me two questions repeatedly: "Why did this happen to Damian?" and "Why did this happen to me?" Of course, Miguel knew there were no answers to these questions. We talked about the uncertainty of life. We talked about his spiritual beliefs. He shared memories of his favorite times with Damian. He continued to suffer.

During our conversations, Miguel talked about how much he wanted this pain to go away. He questioned whether he would ever have a sense of closure and if that was even possible. He talked about what kind of closure might actually be helpful for him in coping with his pain. He knew that even if revenge on the drunk driver were possible, it would ultimately be an empty victory and wouldn't bring Damian back to him. But what would help? An explanation of why the accident happened? He didn't think anything could possibly explain a tragedy like this anyway. Would acceptance of Damian's death provide closure? Miguel was not far enough along in his grief process to consider acceptance. Living his own life in a way that would honor the legacy of his friend? Maybe, but not yet. Closure remained elusive.

I have had similar conversations with clients who have experienced other losses that left them in deep emotional pain. Jobs and romantic relationships are the most common examples, but many of my clients are living with chronic and catastrophic health conditions, and that can also result in emotional pain born from the knowledge that your life is being interrupted and drastically altered. Future plans suddenly derailed. Learning to live with limitations. Insecurity about the future. Fears about how the diagnosis will impact your loved ones, maybe worrying about whether they will accept your diagnosis's impact on their own lives or decide to cut ties with you and move on.

I have also worked with clients who lost a loved one to suicide. They were literally incapacitated by the emotional pain they felt. And they were desperate for closure, caught in the trap of rumination and second-guessing, questioning whether they had been kind and loving and supportive enough, analyzing comments their loved one had made that they now feared were intended to be cries for help. They wanted closure not only to try to understand why their loved one had made this decision but also to help absolve themselves of their intense guilt. This kind of pain can be unbearable, and the impossibility of closure only makes it worse.

EXERCISE:
LISTENING TO YOUR INNER VOICE

Find a quiet place free of distractions and potential interruptions. Sit upright in a comfortable position, not stiff, not slouching, so that you have full access to your breath. Take a few calming breaths, in through the nose, out through the mouth. Deep breaths, not too fast, not too slow—follow your normal breathing, but breathe fully.

With your eyes half-open, look at a point on the wall in front of you (not out a window where you might see something distracting). Think about someone you would like to speak with who could help you with your pain. This might be a person you've lost, someone wise that you currently have in your life, or someone from the past or the present whom you particularly admire. Visualize pouring your heart out to them about your emotional pain. Don't hesitate to tell them all your feelings, plus your thoughts and observations about how you're feeling and why.

What facial expressions does this person have as you tell your story? What words of support do they offer? Is there any advice they might give you to help you find closure? Ask yourself: How can another person help me to heal? And also ask yourself: How can I help myself to heal? Take some time to write down the message you gave yourself. What did you learn from listening to your inner voice?

Childhood Trauma and Closure

I can't talk about closure as a means of healing hurt without discussing the pain of childhood trauma that has been carried into adulthood.

We tend to idealize childhood. The wonders of imagination and discovery. Loving parents. Happy birthday parties with friends. Dance lessons and sports. It's magical, right? Does that describe your childhood? It sure doesn't describe the childhoods of many of the adults who sit on the other side of the tissue box in my office. I think it's safe to say that it isn't easy for all of us to grow up. It wasn't easy for me, and it may not have been for you.

We may accumulate a lot of damage during the process of growing up. In the mental health profession, we often talk about the deep psychological wounds that result from one-time traumatic events, such as the death of a parent, a natural disaster, or a physical or sexual assault. And I have had my share of those conversations. A traumatic event like these can do unfathomable damage to a developing brain. However, I also want to emphasize the potential damage that a steady drip-drip-drip of daily verbal or physical abuse, disrespect, microaggressions, racism, homophobia, bullying, and other forms of pain can do to a developing brain. Experiencing day-to-day acts of unkindness or downright abuse can be increasingly destructive of one's mental health over time, creating deep emotional damage. These daily exposures to acts of abuse can have a cumulative effect with profound results.

When childhood trauma, in whatever form, leaves us with lots of emotional damage, we are also left with questions about what we can do to make the pain go away. Here's where closure enters the picture.

The human mind creates a story for us based on the damage that was done to us. And it tells us that we can make the pain go away, maybe even make sense of what was done to us, by re-creating the story in the present but giving it a happier ending. If we can't fix what happened in the past, maybe we can fix it in the present. So we take the situations that left us with deep wounds in childhood, and we reenact similar situations as adults, usually without realizing it, with the goal of having things turn out "right" this time.

If that happened, we feel, consciously or subconsciously, we would have closure. Finally, the situation would be "fixed" in some way. Most likely, however, we don't get the new ending we want, and we end up continuing to feel the same emotions we were trying to avoid or resolve. And so we give it another try. We live out a new version of the drama, the abuse, the misery that results, hoping that *this* time we'll get an ending so satisfying that all the other bad experiences will fade away as distant memories, never to cause us pain again. We'll get closure.

You've probably heard the line about how the definition of insanity is doing the same thing over and over and expecting different results. It's probably kind of funny the first time you hear it. But if you're a mental health professional, it's a very sad example of something we often witness our clients doing in their lives. I'll give you a few examples of stories that my clients have brought to my office.

- Theo grew up with a distant, withholding, hypercritical father. As an adult, he attached himself to women who were—you guessed it—distant, withholding, and hypercritical. When he came to see me, he was lamenting that the latest woman he dated never appreciated him for who he was or connected with him on an emotional level. He asked me to explain why this always happened to him.

- Tanya grew up as a shy, studious girl who was never really part of a social group and was instead often made fun of and even bullied. She always wanted to be accepted by the more popular girls. As an adult, she tried to make friends with a group of women at work who everyone considered the up-and-coming power players in the company. She told me how they hadn't exactly been open to including her at lunch or happy hours and how they have even directed a few snarky comments toward her.

- Cheri's mother wanted her to be the best. Every day, she told Cheri she had to be better. If Cheri got a B+, it should have been an A. If she came in second place, it should have been first. As an adult, Cheri pushed herself to the limit in her work. She never felt she was good enough—or that anyone else was, much to the frustration of her coworkers. She asked me what she needed to do to get the recognition she deserved at her job. She was considering leaving her company out of frustration. Again.

- Don grew up in a community that valued hypermasculinity. His father and older brothers, as well as his classmates, expected him to join them in hunting and sports, even though he enjoyed reading and the arts. He was repeatedly bullied, beaten up by classmates, and berated by his brothers and their father. He constantly criticized himself for being weak and felt he deserved the abuse he received. Don recently lost another job for creating a toxic workplace by yelling at and threatening the employees he managed. He didn't understand why his strong leadership was being punished.

Each of these individuals has a story they're trying to rewrite: *If I finally do this, say that, hear XYZ, then the past will finally be in the past. Those hard feelings will go away. The voices of criticism, the bullying, the rejection, the pain, the guilt—whatever residual impact is persisting—will finally be quiet. I'll finally have closure.*

These stories from our past are often rehearsed in our minds, over and over. We imagine what it will be like when an emotionally distant, withholding person tells us how wonderful we are and how they can't live without us and how much they want to be with us. Or when people who just don't get how interesting or competent we are finally tell us how much they want us in their social circle or reward us with a promotion. Or when the people who told us we were somehow wrong or not normal show us honor, respect, and deference.

Now, some of us had happier childhoods than others, and most of us have at least some happy memories from our early lives. But even happy memories can get us stuck in the loop of trying to rewrite a story. For example, you might have tried to reexperience happy childhood feelings in romantic relationships, in an attempt to finally be as happy as you once were in your life. *Can't I get that back?* You might hope that getting this type of closure will reaffirm that you really did deserve to be happy, or that experiencing this happiness with a new person will help preserve the memory of someone from your past. Or maybe you have felt guilt over the years for not being as grateful as you should have been in the past, and you resolve that this time around you will fully appreciate your happiness, be grateful for it, not let it slip away.

I refer to this phenomenon as "the closure fantasy"—the ultimate reward for suffering the accumulation of pain that began during childhood. Some mental health professionals might argue about the terminology I'm using, depending on their therapeutic orientation. However, for me, attempting to break the cycle of childhood abuse being repeated in adulthood is, at its heart, all about closure. Finally making it all better. And isn't that what we hope closure will do?

There is something primal and essential about this closure fantasy we walk around with, but it is also on some level simplistic and not based in reality. I have often had clients describe to me exactly what it will look like when they finally have closure, when they finally receive respect, love, inclusion, or whatever else they feel life has up to now denied them. This fantasy scene is not only irrational and unnecessary for your emotional health but it also can cause more damage due to the cycle of defeat, disappointment, and disempowerment that follows.

EXERCISE:
SOOTHING YOUR INNER CHILD

Most of us didn't have a storybook childhood, and many of us still have leftover pain. Under what circumstances is your childhood pain most likely to become stirred up? What triggers you or pushes your buttons?

Think about the last time you felt out of control emotionally. Were the feelings familiar? Do you remember the first time you felt that way? If you take the time to think through this, you will most likely be able to connect current out-of-control feelings to the way you felt as a child when you were misunderstood, not allowed to express yourself, punished, bullied, or when you otherwise experienced any of the childhood events that find a way into our lives as adults.

Now think about how to soothe yourself when these feelings are stirred up. What can you say to yourself to feel grounded? What can you do for yourself to connect with your center? Who can you call to help you to sort out your feelings? Have a self-soothing tool kit in mind that you can use when you need to. Start this process before you reach out to someone to find closure; the closure may be within.

The Power of Stories

What's your story? We all have one. Stories are part of being human. They can empower us to choose to live differently, to not repeat the past, to not be destroyed by holding on to the pain. They can motivate us to repeat the acts of kindness and moments of inspiration we've witnessed, driving us toward productive, happy, successful lives. Or they can trap us in a cycle of playing out the same self-destructive behavior over and over again.

So I don't personally define insanity as doing the same thing over and over and expecting different results. I call that having a story. And all too often, our stories constantly intrude into our lives and repeat the same emotional damage, leaving us with familiar but nonetheless devastating pain and, in the process, keeping us stuck on a treadmill going nowhere.

No, that's not insanity. That's being human.

What I'm essentially saying here is that trying to heal the past through your actions in the present is tough, especially when you're depending on the actions of other people to help you. (See chapter 2 for my speech about how we can't control other people, and how trying to control them never actually leads to closure.) Speaking as a mental health professional, the way to heal from the past is to do the work to deal with what happened in the past. To bravely allow yourself to look at what happened to you, to identify the feelings you experienced, to explore the roles of the people who caused you pain and the role that you played, intentionally or unintentionally. That's hard work. But it is the work required for true closure or acceptance. It begins and ends with you, not with re-creating an experience in the present to try to heal the pain from the past.

It is not my intention to imply that attempting to find closure as a way of healing childhood emotional wounds is a fool's errand. I have witnessed clients finding their way to relationships that finally provide the evidence that they can live a different way, be treated a different way, build the future they dreamed about. It can happen. Are the demons of the past still hovering in the background? Probably. But those clients are able to live in the present and continue to thrive.

However, all too often, I witness clients going through the same dance, over and over, with the same unhappy results. Until they address the issue within themselves, constantly giving their power to another person and asking that person to fix them is only going to leave them back at square one. If you find yourself in that position, is it time to consider giving up the fight and refocusing on understanding the voices inside of you telling you how worthless, unlovable, or incompetent you are? In other words, the next time the same music starts playing, is it time to start singing a different song?

I frequently look for these kinds of stories when I'm working with clients. Sometimes the story emerges into the light so that we can examine it together; sometimes it doesn't. Either way, I think it's an important discussion to help clients gain clarity with themselves on what is holding them back. No one is trapped in the past, destined to repeat it over and over, unless they allow themselves to be.

SELF-ASSESSMENT: BEFORE YOU SEEK CLOSURE

As you consider the potential benefits and drawbacks of seeking closure to heal unrelenting emotional pain, here are some questions to ask yourself.

- Why do I feel this way? What do I think is the source of my pain?

- Am I seeking closure in a way that will directly address my source of pain?
- Was a feeling or memory from the past brought up, and is it something I need to address in another way?
- Is the intensity of my feeling appropriate to the situation?
- Exactly what would closure need to look like if my pain is going to be relieved?
- Is my approach to gaining closure likely to result in the closure I want?
- Is this person/entity realistically able to give me closure?
- Is it possible the closure I am seeking will feel like an empty victory?
- Will this closure be enough to make all the pain go away? Some of it?
- Am I prepared to cope if I don't receive the closure I want?

Taking the time to consider these questions can help you be more aware of what you can expect, and not expect, and to protect yourself from further pain.

Closing Thought: Suffering Is Human

Remember the character of the Tin Man in *The Wizard of Oz*? At the end of the movie, when Dorothy presents the Tin Man with a ticking watch, he says he knows he has a heart now because it's breaking. How many other movies, songs, and books have been written about the pain of a broken heart? The greater message here is that having a broken heart is human.

It has been my experience that one of the main causes of emotional pain is an inability or refusal to accept what happened or, to put it more directly, a refusal to accept reality. When you can't or won't face the reality of a situation, you set up a battle in your own mind. The purely emotional side of your mind fights it out with the rational side of your mind. What's the result? More pain. We will focus more on the role of acceptance in part 4. Closure may provide you with what you need to hear to help you accept things as they are and move on. Or it may not.

We look to closure to heal our emotional pain. We hope for words, actions, or divine interventions to provide the endpoint of our pain and the beginning of what we hope or pray will be a way forward. It's only human to want our pain to come to an end. To want closure. Sometimes the closure that occurs is indeed magical. Other times it's just a hope, a dream, a fantasy.

Chapter 4

We're Angry

Feelings of anger are closely related to feelings of pain, and like feelings of pain, they're a common motivation for seeking closure. When we feel we have been emotionally or otherwise injured by another person, it is only human to feel angry as well as hurt. We all get angry from time to time—or a lot of the time. Feelings of anger can motivate a desire for closure in both healthy and unhealthy ways. You might want to resolve angry feelings simply by talking them out calmly—or you might want to make sure the other person knows how mad you are, to tell them off, to make them give you the apology you deserve.

Before I talk about anger and its relationship with closure, I'd like to take a step back and look more closely at the role of anger in modern life. You might agree with me that we live in a culture of anger. We see it everywhere. In the news. In the workplace. On the sidewalk. In stores and restaurants. In traffic. At family get-togethers. You might have had the experience, as I have, of having a perfectly civil conversation with a friendly, mannered person and then, when politics or social issues find their way into the conversation, observed their face contort with rage, followed by a few expletives you weren't quite expecting. I certainly see a lot of anger in my line of work. Some of my clients are just seething with anger or have had seething anger directed toward them, and they're looking to me to help them change, or cope, or both.

Having said this, I want to acknowledge that anger can be a force for positive change. For example, anger has helped people organize forces for needed social reforms around the globe. Anger has caused oppressed people to fight for their rights. It has led to resources being directed to people who need them, and the creation of new resources. It has led to increased awareness of economic or health disparities when someone finally got mad enough to sound an alarm.

I can also vouch for the role of anger in motivating individual change. I have clients who, because they finally acknowledged their anger at the situation they were in, felt ready to take the risks required to find a new way to live. Admitting to themselves that their current job or career was creating misery. That a relationship was not supportive, or wasn't making them happy, or was downright abusive or toxic. That current lifestyles, like unhealthy eating habits or substance abuse, needed to change. Clients allowed themselves to feel their anger at an aspect of their life, channeled that anger into positive energy, and moved forward.

So yes, anger can have its upsides. But on a day-to-day level, the increase in rage is alarming. I'm not trying to be a doomsayer, but from what I observe, it seems that the rise in anger in the world has no end in sight. Anger has become a default emotion, if not *the* default emotion, in the world we live in.

Anger as a Covering Emotion

Anger often starts small, as resentment. The resentment you feel when, after you've labored long and hard, an expected promotion is offered to someone else. The resentment you feel when a valued professional relationship is damaged due to a coworker's lack of attention. The resentment you feel when your partner appears to be less committed to your happiness and peace of mind than you are to theirs. The resentment you feel when you find out about a family or friend get-together to which you were not invited. Resentment can build over time, or it can erupt into anger suddenly.

Anger makes us want to do something, to take action. It's only human to want to do something with our angry or resentful feelings, to let them out, to make them go away. Anger eats at us unmercifully, makes it hard to be productive, damages relationships, pushes people away, and does harm to our emotional and physical health. Consequently, it is completely logical that anger would motivate us to seek closure. *I need to do something to make this anger go away!*

I think it's important to take a step back and give you some background on the psychology of anger here. Anger is a primary emotion, meaning it's fundamental, instantaneous, visceral. Something happens that we don't like, and boom! We get mad.

But anger can also be a "covering emotion." Let me explain what I mean by that. Have you ever felt overwhelmingly sad, just crushed by your sadness . . . and then found yourself getting angry as a way to avoid feeling the depth of that sadness? That's one way anger can be used as a covering emotion. We use it to protect ourselves from feelings that are especially hard to sit with, like sadness, pain, and fear. We get angry in order to put up a shield that protects others from getting too close to our tender side, the side that feels sad, afraid, wounded.

For example, I often hear about angry feelings when I'm speaking with a client about a breakup. They are hurt and sad, but they can't acknowledge that yet. I have to help them sort through the anger, to let those angry feelings find their way out into the open, before they can begin to look at how hurt they are. As another example, it may be hard to look at how fearful we feel in the event of a job loss. We may be terrified of losing our livelihood or not being able to support our families. It's hard to face that fear and the helplessness that can accompany it. It's a lot easier to express all that as rage at your former employer.

Anger is so useful as a covering emotion that when I was doing postgraduate training at the Albert Ellis Institute here in New York, I once actually approached one of the instructors and asked him if anger was, in fact, *always* a way of covering other emotions. I still remember his answer. He said, "Gary, have you ever taken a bottle away from a baby?" I answered, "Certainly not." He said, "Well, if you do, you'll hear a lot of screaming. That baby is pretty mad." Anger *is* a primary emotion. And it's also a covering emotion.

My point here is that it's really important to take a look at your anger before you seek closure. To understand the source of your anger. And to make your intentions clear to yourself so that you can make your intentions clear to the person from whom you're seeking closure. (You'll read more on the topic of intentionality in part 3 of this book.) If you seek closure without taking the time to understand what you're angry about and whether it's really anger you need to gain closure on or other feelings that you aren't allowing into your awareness, you may end up doing damage to a relationship, your own emotional wellness, or both. I think it's safe to say that venting your anger at someone when it's actually intense sadness or fear you're feeling will not leave you in a better place emotionally.

How Anger Motivates the Quest for Closure

Think about the last time you were angry about something. Take a moment and really feel that anger. This might take some work, but if you're like most people, you can easily access memories of frustrating events in your life and the angry feelings that resulted from them. Many of my clients tell me that feeling angry is all too easy, that these memories are always on the surface, ready to be brought back to life by events that occur in the present. In fact, you may currently be in the midst of a situation in your life that is causing you great anger, and for which you are hoping to find some kind of closure to heal your angry feelings.

As you experience these angry feelings, ask yourself: *How would closure help me find some kind of healing for my anger?* The following are some of the most common desired outcomes when we seek closure that is motivated by anger.

To Feel Understood

One of the most frustrating things in life is to feel misunderstood or, worse yet, not heard at all. When we feel that another person is not understanding our point of view, we just can't help wanting to find a way to make that person "get" us. This can become an obsession. It grates on you, eats at you. *That person needs to understand why I'm mad! Then I'll feel closure!*

It follows that your expectation of closure might revolve around a conversation. You might want to sit down with the person who has caused your anger and explain to them why you feel so angry. You might hope they follow with an explanation of how they feel, which might lead to more discussion, more back and forth, to create understanding.

If all goes well, seeking closure to gain understanding can be a real relationship builder. You can learn about the person from whom you're seeking closure, how they respond to anger, how committed they are to maintaining a relationship with you. They may learn something about you too.

Of course, the flip side is that they might not understand your anger. In fact, they might say you're overreacting, confused, being dramatic—which will leave your anger intact, if not at a higher level than when you started. That's the risk of seeking closure to heal your anger through being understood.

To Get an Apology

My clients often talk about the value of an apology in healing their angry feelings. A statement such as "I just want to be understood . . ." is often followed by ". . . and hear them apologize for what they did." When someone does something that causes us harm, emotional or otherwise, we want an apology from them. We want to know they take responsibility and acknowledge what they did to cause our anger.

The good news is that people can and sometimes will take in your angry feelings, hear you out, and apologize. They may begin to apologize as soon as they see how angry you are, realizing that what they did had unintended consequences. Or they may need to clearly hear from you what made you angry, why you're reacting this way, and the impact their words or actions had on you. In either case, an apology can bring you closer and deepen your relationship.

On the other hand, the other person may refuse to take responsibility, saying the whole situation is your fault. Or they may say they see no problem at all and "so why are you so angry?" Or they may give you a Mona Lisa smile and say something like "Sorry you feel that way." In these cases, you might end up even angrier than when you started.

To Get Revenge

We're human. Our motives aren't always pure. When an emotional button gets pushed, rational thinking can fly out the window. They pushed our buttons, and we want to push theirs in return. We may not even be aware that's what's happening.

Let's say you learn you weren't invited to a friend's birthday party, and man oh man, are you mad about it. You decide you're so mad that your friend needs to know. You wait until the night before the birthday party to give them a call. You tell them you know about the party, that they can't keep it a secret from you. You state how offended and angry you are that they've treated you this way. You know this friend is sensitive and takes things hard, so you can be sure they'll feel too guilty to have a good time at the party the next day.

Tossing an emotional grenade can feel good at the moment, but as we discussed in chapter 2, revenge is not the same thing as closure. And grenades leave a lot of damage behind.

EXERCISE: GETTING OUT ALL THAT ANGER

Clients often ask how to get out all the anger they have bottled up inside in a way that is not going to harm their reputation or relationships. Anger-releasing activities can help you get beyond the initial rush of emotions and take a more rational view of what's bothering you. Think of something you're currently angry about. Now, channel that anger into an activity. Here are some ideas.

- Write a mean letter that you have no intention of sending.
- Slug a pillow.
- Kick a beach ball against a wall, and kick it again when it comes back to you.
- Take a fast walk while giving whoever is involved a piece of your mind (silently if you're around other people, out loud if you're not).
- Find a place where you won't draw attention to yourself or scare anybody and yell some really bad words.
- Ask yourself: How does it feel to let some of this anger out?

Weighing the Risks

As we move forward in this chapter, I want to emphasize that gaining closure to heal angry feelings can build a relationship. Getting the anger and the hurt out can help you and the other person to understand each other better. To watch out for each other's emotions. To be more aware of each other's needs and vulnerabilities. But because we often fear the dark places anger can go, we may miss out on the growth that can be gained by healing anger through closure. So let me repeat that closure can be a powerful tool in healing anger.

As a therapist, I have seen many, many clients finally gain the courage to sit down with a friend, a partner, a family member, or a colleague and seek closure by talking about their angry feelings—and feeling a sense of healing as a result. *Healing* is the operative word here. If you have felt the effects of anger on your emotional and physical wellness, you know what I mean.

But the opposite can be true as well. Take Darryl and Rebecca. The two of them were very close friends, almost inseparable. They talked on the phone daily and had dinner at the same restaurant every Saturday evening. They talked about everything: work, their families, any dating either of them did. Everything.

Darryl was always aware that Rebecca could be difficult at times. She was very direct, sometimes to the point of being harsh, but he chalked that up to her nature and told himself to accept her sometimes barbed and even humiliating comments as evidence she was concerned about him. Rebecca could also be controlling at times, telling Darryl what he should or should not do, and criticizing him when he didn't take her advice. Sometimes she would get angry at him, suddenly and with great force, for something she thought he was doing wrong, like the time she berated him for not suggesting what movie they should see and making her do the heavy lifting in their friendship. She could also be competitive, one-upping him when he told her about an accomplishment or stated an opinion. When she began dating someone, Rebecca would point out Darryl's flaws in front of her new partner, sometimes even making fun of him. Finally, one day, Rebecca called him, accused him of not being a supportive friend, and told him she was taking a break from the relationship.

At first Darryl was sad. He felt he had been a loyal friend and didn't understand her accusation. But as Darryl reflected back on the relationship—the times Rebecca had put him down, embarrassed him by being rude to service people, attempted to tell him what to do, threatened to withhold her friendship if he disappointed her in some way—he began to feel resentment toward her. Followed by anger, lots of anger, as he realized what a toxic presence she had been in his life. Truth be told, Darryl was in a rage when he thought about the time he had spent with Rebecca and what he had put up with.

Yet Darryl was hesitant to have a conversation with Rebecca. He knew she was a much better debater than he was, and he feared that a face-to-face discussion would lead to a verbally adept denial of her behavior and a lecture on his own psychological problems. After all, he had known Rebecca for years. Why would she behave any differently now? How likely was it that they could have a heart-to-heart discussion of their relationship: what had gone well, what had contributed to their falling out, what they each could have done differently, a sharing of happy memories, an exchange of best wishes . . . ? In Darryl's mind, not very likely. In the end, he chose not to pursue a closure conversation with her; instead, he decided to accept the situation for what it was and move on, even though his rage wasn't vented and his questions weren't answered.

When we seek closure with another person, we're asking something of them, whether it's merely to listen or to react in some way. To some degree, you're making your healing dependent upon how the other person chooses to respond to you. This can bring two people together and make their relationship stronger, or it can drive a wedge between them or even end a relationship. It's important to approach any closure conversations with an understanding of these risks.

A Note about Anger at Organizations

Generally, when we look for closure to heal ourselves from anger, we want to go directly to the source of our anger, that person who we view as the cause of the anger. But is the person you have in mind the actual person who caused your anger, or are they representing an organization you're angry with? Are you angry at a specific service worker, or are you angry at your bank, or an airline, or your doctor's office? In other words, are you trying to feel better by dumping on someone else? If you've ever taken out your anger on a customer service representative or receptionist, you might also have noticed that the closure you received was temporary at best, potentially followed by a lot of remorse. And I have had some of those beleaguered service professionals as clients, so I've seen how they end up wanting closure of their own as a result of the hurt and anger customers' mistreatment brings out in them. My point is: Make sure you're clear about the true source of your anger and aren't just raging at someone who isn't actually in a position to give you the closure you want.

SELF-ASSESSMENT: CLOSURE FOR ANGRY FEELINGS

As you consider your need for closure to heal angry feelings, it's important to take the time to gain an understanding of your anger. That means taking a hard look at yourself and asking some uncomfortable questions so that you can approach gaining closure with a rational mind. Here are some questions to ask yourself.

- Why am I so angry?
- Did I play a role here that I don't want to look at?
- Is it really anger I'm feeling, or is it a different feeling I don't want to acknowledge, such as sadness, disappointment, or fear?
- What kind of closure am I expecting? Understanding? Forgiveness?
- Are my motives for closure productive, or do I have some desire to do some damage to the other person?
- What can I reasonably expect from the person I'm seeking closure from?
- Is the intensity of my anger appropriate to the situation, or is it related to a feeling or memory from the past that has been brought up and that I need to address in another way?
- Am I prepared for the possibility that I'll come away from my attempt at closure feeling even more angry?
- Am I trying to gain closure with the person who caused my anger, or is the person the face of an organization that needs to be aware of my anger through other means?

Closing Thought:
Choosing to Do Better

We are often taught that when we have anger toward another person, the healthy thing to do is to sit down with them and talk things out. We learn this from our parents and schoolteachers; we see it in the media. Thinking back, I can say that my first experience with finding closure was in resolving an angry situation in school as a child.

But we also live in a world in which anger is not always resolved through closure—unless you count hateful social media posts, getting revenge, or doing direct damage as closure. I think it's safe to say that much of the anger in the world is not being resolved but rather perpetuated. No, that's not closure.

It's only human to get angry at times, but we get to choose how we deal with it. We can choose to seek closure to heal angry feelings in a way that helps us to grow as individuals and builds relationships, or that allows us to walk away from a relationship with self-respect, respect for the other person, and integrity.

Chapter 5

We Feel Helpless

When was the last time you felt helpless? Life seems to give us daily opportunities to feel helpless. And much like pain and anger, that feeling of helplessness can lead to a desire for, if not an obsession with, closure.

I am addressing helplessness relatively early on in our exploration of closure because my discussions of closure with my clients frequently include talking about their feelings of helplessness. Why this connection? Think of it this way: Almost by definition, the reason you want closure is that you did not have control over a given situation. It didn't play out the way you wanted it to, and you were powerless to change that. That original lack of control creates a desire for resolution, and if you try and fail to get that resolution, it only reminds you of your continued lack of control.

I don't think a week goes by in which I don't talk with a client about their feelings of helplessness. Many of my clients are living with chronic or catastrophic health conditions; some are nearing the ends of their lives. Receiving a medical diagnosis can be one of the most helpless situations you ever encounter. You don't know why it's happening to you. You may have to make major lifestyle

changes that you didn't choose and don't want to make. You may
not know what it means for your future. It's like having an unin-
vited houseguest move in and take control of your home.

I talk with clients about helplessness in other situations as
well. Financial problems that feel unrelenting and unsolvable. A
relationship that may be irreparably damaged. Worries about a
child or other family member who is making bad decisions. Feel-
ing stuck in a miserable job. And on and on. Life seems to give us
all kinds of reasons to feel helpless.

And it is only human to dread feelings of helplessness. We
want to be in control, or at least exercise agency over some of our
decisions. We want to know that if we do *this*, we will get *that*. We
want reassurance that we're on the right path to get what we've
worked for, that doing the right thing is going to give us the payoff
we desire. We don't want to have to deal with bad things, to have
to feel bad feelings. We look to closure to answer questions we
can't answer, hoping that information will make us feel like we're
in the driver's seat. We want closure to absolve us of any past ac-
tions we wish we could change.

Let's start with a small example of helplessness. Imagine that
you're driving to work on the highway during rush hour. Sud-
denly, a car comes up on your left side and swerves in front of you,
cutting you off. You might just roll your eyes and shrug it off,
maybe slowing down to create some distance between you and
the aggressive driver. But what if this incident brought up memo-
ries from your childhood and made you feel like you were being
bullied and disrespected, helpless to protect yourself from some-
body who thought it would be fun to push you around? So you
swerve into the left lane, pull up beside the big bully in the other
car, give the driver the one-finger salute, and cut them off.

Wow! You, the former victim, are finally taking an aggressive
approach and not letting someone else push you around! All those
dangling loose ends of helplessness are momentarily tied into a

firm knot. You finally got closure. Right? And it sure feels good! For the moment . . .

And what about a more significant example of helplessness? Let me tell you about Amelia, a producer for a major TV news network whose job involves managing lots and lots of details. Many are planned and handled ahead of time; others have to be handled as events occur. She loves her work but can get overwhelmed by the stress involved. She often feels like a ringmaster in a three-ring circus, surrounded by lions who are constantly looking for an opening to pounce on her. She believes she is always one error away from damage to her reputation if not the loss of her job.

Last week, one of those dreaded moments occurred. A detail slipped through the cracks during a busy day, and as a result, she missed an opportunity for one of the on-air reporters to interview an important politician. This was a big loss for the show she works on. And all eyes were on her as the person who let the ball drop.

Amelia has felt terrible since this happened. She hasn't slept well for a week. She feels exposed, ashamed, sad. Angry at herself. She's worried this error will never be forgotten or forgiven. She wishes it had never happened, that she could make this go away. She usually prides herself on being in control at all times, but now she feels helpless to fix the damage she caused to her show and to herself.

Her mentor has advised her to hold her head up and get back to work, but Amelia wants closure to make those helpless feelings go away. She has asked for a meeting with the senior producer to do a blow-by-blow of the events leading up to the error. She wants to uncover a missing detail that will explain why this happened, that will make it clear that the circumstances were not normal. At heart, she wants to be absolved, or at least she wants it to be clear that anyone in her position could have made this error. In other words, she wants her senior producer to give her the closure she needs.

Helplessness makes us feel trapped. Closure can feel like a way out of the trap.

EXERCISE:
HOW HAVE YOU COPED WITH HELPLESSNESS?

Think back to a time in your life when you felt helpless about something that happened to you or to another person, and consider the following questions. Don't use this as an avenue for self-criticism; we do the best we can at the time with what we know and the resources we have available.

- In this situation, what feelings came up for you?
- How did you cope with your feelings?
- Did these feelings lead to you shutting down?
- Did these feelings lead to you taking action?
- Looking back, is there anything you might have done differently in response to your helplessness?
- Have you gained any insights into your approach to coping with helplessness?

What If I Pretend Everything's Okay?

In working with my clients, I have learned a lot about the ways in which they cope, or don't cope, with feelings of helplessness. People often go to great lengths to completely deny these feelings. One obvious example, given the nature of my work with individuals living with chronic conditions, is clients who refuse to own their diagnosis and receive the appropriate treatment, or who take medication but refuse to consider the lifestyle changes they need to make to maintain their wellness. Another example of denial might be someone who refuses to acknowledge their partner is cheating on them, despite clear evidence. Ah, denial. *If I pretend it's not there, I won't have to feel helpless.* But of course, life doesn't work that way.

Denial is often tied up with a desire for closure. This is based on a simple logic: *If you say or do the thing I want you to say or do, then I won't have to feel any responsibility or be forced to admit to myself that I have no control.*

For example, my client Mina talked to me about how her partner, Dominic, decided to move across the country from New York to Los Angeles. He did not ask her to accompany him. She felt that Dominic needed to focus on his career, that this was an opportunity he couldn't turn down, and that he needed to use all his time and energy on being successful in this job. Mina was very clear about the closure she needed. She needed a "Yes, I want to build a life together in Los Angeles" or a "No, I need to put my career first and don't see a place for you in my life."

Now, I had been having conversations with Mina about her relationship for a long while. Dominic, from my perspective, seemed to be having quite a few meetings that kept him from being home in the evenings, not to mention a frequent need to be away on the weekends. Based on what Mina told me, he seemed to be avoiding her. But Mina had been in complete denial of the problems in her relationship. If she admitted to the problems they were having, she would also have to admit those problems couldn't have anything to do with Dominic's waning interest in her. That would mean looking at her own role in the relationship problems, which she didn't want to have to do, as well as her lack of control over Dominic's level of commitment. She couldn't sit with the feelings of helplessness as their relationship gradually crumbled.

Getting the closure Mina thought she needed would place the blame for the breakup on Dominic's career opportunity, not on any part either of them played in the deterioration of the relationship. She could live with that. It would let her stay in denial about how their relationship was falling apart and how she was helpless to fix it. The closure Mina wanted was one that would keep her fear of helplessness at a distance.

Have you ever felt so afraid of sitting with your essential help-lessness, your complete inability to change a situation, that you longed for another person to give you closure that would keep those helpless feelings away? Even if it meant denying a hard truth that in your heart of hearts you know you are going to have to face some day?

If so, you're human. And it's only human nature to do just about anything to avoid feeling helpless.

Don't I Matter?

Not feeling validated can bring up feelings of helplessness, be-cause invalidation is disempowering. Take a moment to think about all the ways in which you might be validated on an average day. Your partner wishes you a good morning. You receive a text message or an email with a response to a request you made. Some-body holds the door for you as you walk into your place of work. A friend or family member invites you to an upcoming birthday party. A service worker thanks you for your business. As you read through these examples, your brain may be conjuring up even more.

You might also be thinking *Hmm . . . I never thought of that as validation.* That's because we tend to take these kinds of everyday validation for granted. Validation often happens on an uncon-scious level. We give it. We receive it. Whether we notice it or not depends on factors like how much we value the relationship, what kind of mood we're in, and what else is on our mind. We don't necessarily take the time to question how to validate another per-son, nor do we take the time to consider whether we have been validated. It's just a normal part of our daily routine as we interact in the world. Feeling validated, even if we're not consciously aware of it, provides us with a sense of normalcy, along with evidence that the world is safe and welcoming.

Until, that is, we feel we haven't been validated when we should have been. This can be subtle. Validation comes to us in the form of words, facial expressions, body language, and acts of respect or kindness. Consequently, we can feel invalidated when one or more of these elements are missing, intentionally or unintentionally. Perhaps a coworker is distracted, unhelpful, neglects to say thank you. You might just roll your eyes and assume they're having a bad day. Or you might try to have a conversation—or give them a piece of your mind. You might try to tie up those loose ends one way or another.

But it's the bigger invalidations, not the everyday ones, that people usually come to me to talk about. A big invalidation occurs when, for example, your partner tells you they don't have the time or energy to listen to you talk about something that happened at work. Or you get left off your friend's birthday party guest list. Or a family member refuses to treat you like a grown-up and instead patronizes or humiliates you, just to remind you of where you stand.

I'll tell you about Robert, a man in his forties who is very close to his siblings and extended family. He likes to think of himself as instrumental in keeping the family in contact with each other. He always chooses the venues for the various get-togethers they have around the holidays, and he doesn't mind doing the traveling if others can't or don't want to travel.

One year, his sister mentioned they should plan a family reunion in July. Robert loved the idea. After some research, he decided that they should meet in the town where his grandmother lived, since she would have difficulty traveling. He remembered a park near her had a great covered pavilion and he made a reservation. But before he had the time to let everybody know what he was planning, he received a card in the mail from his sister announcing the first annual family reunion in his sister's town and telling everyone to save the date.

Robert was shocked. He hadn't even been consulted. He felt invalidated by his sister and, by extension, his other family members. Was all the work he had done over the years to keep them all connected worth nothing to them?

I don't know anyone on the planet who hasn't at one time or another felt invalidated by another person—a family member, a friend, a romantic partner. I sure have! How do we gain closure in these situations? And what about a relationship in which you have felt invalidated repeatedly over time? I suspect that as you read this chapter, you may remember times when you felt invalidated, along with the feelings of helplessness that often accompany invalidation. *Am I invisible? Am I unloved? Not valued?* Wanting to answer these questions drives the need for closure.

EXERCISE:
WHAT DO I NEED FROM OTHER PEOPLE?

Ever have that nagging feeling that you aren't being noticed, acknowledged, or heard? If so, you may relate to a lot of what I've written in this chapter. So how about getting specific with yourself?

What specific kinds of validation do you want or like to receive from other people? Someone holding the door for you? Coworkers asking for help with something you're good at? Words of kindness and appreciation from your partner, a friend, or a family member? Sit down with yourself and think about what makes you feel validated. Make a list. Ask yourself: Am I expecting things that the people in my life can actually deliver? Are there times when I'm expecting too much? Are there times when I'm not expecting enough?

Think about what you can expect and not expect from the people in your life. You may need to narrow the list down to what makes rational sense. And then over the coming weeks, take time to validate other people the same ways you like to be validated. Validating other people has its own rewards. And see what comes back to you.

It Just Doesn't Make Sense

Our innate need to *know* can also leave us feeling helpless. When things don't go as expected, we want answers. Open loops have to be closed. And so we pursue closure. But that very natural inclination is all too often confounded by the essential unpredictability of humans. In my experience working with my clients, I've found that even the most predictable of people can surprise us, in good ways and in not-so-good ways.

Making sense of another person's actions can be a double whammy when seeking closure. We may want answers about their treatment of us, actions they took that caused us emotional harm, and yet when we try to find closure, not only do we *not* find those answers, but their response to us confuses us even more! When you're in this position, it's all too easy to become obsessed with closing that loop. You might doggedly keep after the other person, having repeat conversations, trying to make sense out of it all. "Why did you do that?" "What were you thinking?" "Didn't you care about how that might affect me?"

Unfortunately, this often results in further confusion and frustration. It also puts you in a position of disempowerment, because you're relying on the other person to explain things to you. You've essentially made your peace of mind dependent upon the actions of another person. I'm not saying that seeking closure is inherently disempowering. Not at all. But I am saying that attempting to resolve your own helpless feelings by depending on another person's actions can leave you feeling even more helpless.

Here's an example. Maggie and Susanah were practically inseparable. Not only had they worked together day and night to build their business, but also they were best friends. Sure, they had some bumps along the way, but they always worked it out—until Susanah went behind Maggie's back and made a business deal to create a new company that Maggie would not be a part of. This for Maggie was a betrayal that she never imagined would happen. Maggie felt she couldn't rest until she understood why Susanah chose to behave this way.

She approached Susanah a few times to talk this out. Susanah told her repeatedly that it was an opportunity she couldn't turn down. When Maggie asked, "But what about me? What about us?" Susanah just shrugged. Maggie isn't sure what answer Susanah could have given that would help her make sense of an action that came out of left field. Instead of finding peace, Maggie actually felt more and more frustrated, angry, and powerless. But she couldn't give up.

Have you ever tried to find closure with someone who couldn't seem to give you a reasonable explanation of why they behaved as they did? Did you feel helpless as a result? As I have often said to my clients, we aren't always going to understand why someone decides to cheat or lie or otherwise betray us. We aren't always going to understand why we don't get a job we were totally qualified for or an award we deserved. We aren't always going to understand why someone we think we can trust suddenly turns on us and behaves in a way we never would have expected. We aren't always going to understand why someone doesn't love us the way we want them to.

And most heartbreaking of all, we aren't always going to understand why someone we love loses their life. Even when death makes logical sense, as when someone passes from old age, it often doesn't make *emotional* sense. The unanswered questions can leave us feeling helpless.

We're human. We can't stand to not understand. We have to make sense of things. But the sad and hard truth is that as long as you continue to demand sense when no sense is forthcoming, you are creating your own suffering and, ironically, increasing your sense of helplessness. In that way, the desire for closure can be a trap. You can find yourself in an existential temper tantrum, metaphorically lying on your back, kicking and screaming, demanding that life make sense, that your questions be answered, that you get to walk away feeling calm, satisfied, enlightened, and most of all, no longer in pain.

And so often the existential temper tantrum is not about understanding the mysteries of life but rather understanding them *on your terms*, based on other people's faults and errors, not yours. This is not meant to sound harsh or judgmental. The existential temper tantrum is a demand for meaning in a world where there often is no greater meaning other than the fact that people are scrambling about trying to do their best and falling short. They are, we are, most likely you are. To be human is to be flawed and, consequently, to hurt others. And sometimes we're helpless to make sense of it.

SELF-ASSESSMENT: FEELINGS OF HELPLESSNESS

Asking yourself questions is a great way to gain insight and self-awareness. Here are some questions to ask yourself to better understand any feelings of helplessness you might be having and how these feelings may be impacting your desire for closure. Some of these questions may be painful to con-sider or contemplate. They are not intended to be confron-tational or otherwise imply that you are without emotional coping skills. But I am a big believer in asking the hard ques-tions. Self-awareness is power! It is the beginning of making choices in life that benefit yourself and those around you.

- Do I feel like I am backed into a corner or trapped?
- Is just feeling better all that's important to me right now?
- Do I feel that I don't have my own resources to make myself feel better?
- Am I frequently saying to myself, "If only XYZ would happen . . ."?
- Is my mind constantly conjuring up scenarios that are alternatives to what really happened?
- Do I feel that another person holds the key to helping me find hope again?
- Am I telling myself that my life may not get any better if I don't get the closure I need?
- Do I find myself ruminating on what someone else could do or say to make me feel better?
- How can seeking closure to resolve my feelings of invalidation benefit our relationship? Or damage it? And am I willing to take that risk?
- What are the potential ways the other person may react when I approach them to talk about my feelings of helplessness?
- Can I cope emotionally with each possible outcome? Do I have the necessary support I might need to help me cope?

- Is it possible that I need to look within myself to resolve these feelings of helplessness rather than seeking closure with this person?

Using Closure as a Weapon

Closure motivated by the desire to deny feelings of powerlessness can become an agenda, a carefully formulated plan to move a situation in the direction that benefits you the most or to get another person to do what you want them to do. Attempting to hold other people to your own agenda can be destructive. It can lead to results you didn't intend, such as the loss of a relationship or stronger feelings of helplessness than you started out with. It can even become a weapon.

I have had clients on both sides of this dynamic: those who used closure as a weapon and those who had closure used as a weapon against them. Clients who were invited to have a conversation about the past, only for the other person to use that conversation as an opportunity to do more harm. Clients who have had another person repeatedly hold out on them, saying they were willing to talk but then refusing—a carrot and a stick. When the closure you are seeking is being weaponized, against you or against someone else, then you're headed toward further disempowerment.

My client Thanh, for example, was bullied in high school by the "in-group." One of the chief bullies contacted him years later, brought up examples of ways in which he had hurt Thanh, and asked for forgiveness, which Thanh granted. Afterward, though, Thanh wasn't sure if, on balance, he felt any better. On one hand, he had the apology he'd always thought he deserved. On the other hand, the exchange brought up a lot of bad memories for him, and he felt a rush of difficult emotions.

Although the high school bully professed that he regretted his actions, Thanh had to grapple with the reminder of the anger and fear he'd experienced in high school, how powerless he'd felt to defend himself, and how he had carried this damage with him into adulthood. He was left wondering if this was essentially a new opportunity for the bully to assert power over him by placing himself in the position of having decided to "grant" Thanh closure. Was this just one more power play? Whatever the bully's true intentions, Thanh felt that the closure being offered was more like a weapon being used to stir up past hurt.

The high school bully followed up by inviting Thanh to take part in a Facebook group from their old high school, saying he was sure other classmates would want to be back in touch with him. Thanh joined and immediately felt like he was back in high school with the same group of students, now middle-aged. He was overcome with memories of their unkind comments and exclusionary cliques as they posted fond reminiscences of events that were painful for him.

So while the bully who contacted him may have felt some closure, Thanh did not. He had to question the intentions behind the apology he had received if this person hadn't considered how stirring up these memories and inviting him to the Facebook group might affect him. The past was brought into the present, and closure felt like the weapon being used to bring more pain.

Closing Thought:
Feeling Helpless Is Human

"Man plans. God laughs." Have you heard that expression? It summarizes well the human condition. And it summarizes closure that is motivated by helplessness. We want to control what happens in our lives. We want to avoid hard and painful feelings. We want to know why! The alternative is to feel helpless.

But most of life is out of our control. Regrettably, it just is. Consequently, a key to contentment is recognizing our lack of control and accepting that reality. When we accept the places where we don't have control, we are in a much better position to recognize the places where we *do* have control and to make the best of the control we have.

Sitting with helplessness means sitting with uncomfortable feelings. It means accepting that so much of life is out of our control, as much as we would wish otherwise. But it also means you can stop fighting futile battles. And when you do, you empower yourself to take control where you can, to move forward in life.

What does this mean for closure? It means accepting where you can get closure and where you can't. It means using your rational mind to seek closure in a way that is appropriate to the situation, based on a realistic appraisal of what is possible and what is not. To seek closure in a way that is empowering, that does not diminish yourself by attempting to control the other person or giving them power over your own emotional wellness. That is healthy closure.

Chapter 6

We Want Forgiveness

eelings of pain, anger, and helplessness are often the motivation behind the quest for closure. Heartbreakingly often, so is a desire for forgiveness. We may want forgiveness for what we feel were destructive actions on our part, or we may want someone else to recognize what they did wrong and to seek our forgiveness. Either way, seeking forgiveness can lead to very needed and beneficial closure—or it can leave us trapped in an unending cycle, seeking closure that remains elusive.

"I'm sorry."

"I apologize."

"Please forgive me."

You might agree with me that these are some of the most profound words in the English language. It can be hard to say these words. It can be equally hard to hear these words. As you read those words, did any memories come up for you—times when you were on the giving or receiving end of a conversation about forgiveness? When you consider those memories, what kinds of emotions come up for you? I suspect all kinds of feelings—sad, angry, bittersweet. Forgiveness can be straightforward, but it can also be complicated, emotionally and mentally.

It's Hard to Say "I'm Sorry"

To fully explore forgiveness as a motivation for seeking closure, I want to begin by talking about why it's so hard to ask for forgiveness.

Humans have a basic need to be right. We don't like to admit that we made an error. We don't want to think of ourselves as mean-spirited, incompetent, forgetful, or in possession of any number of real or perceived flaws that might place us in the position of needing to ask someone else for forgiveness. We just plain don't like to admit that we committed a transgression against someone else. Admitting you were wrong may also mean admitting that the other person was right. This might all add up to having to face the fact that we aren't perfect.

But that's why, as hard as it may be, asking for forgiveness can be freeing. It allows us to come to terms with our own lack of perfection and humanity. Asking for forgiveness can finally help to address the rift in a relationship that may be resulting from whatever transgression has been committed. In fact, asking for forgiveness for our mistakes can open the door to the other person seeking forgiveness for their own mistakes. The healing that can result benefits the person seeking forgiveness, the person granting forgiveness, and the relationship between them.

So what gets in the way?

Let's not underestimate the role of our egos. Asking for forgiveness is humbling. We may perceive it as a blow to our self-esteem, or it may feel like bringing ourselves down in order to build someone else up, giving the other person the upper hand at our own expense. If you're already suffering, your ego may be feel-

WE WANT FORGIVENESS ■ 71

ing especially fragile, and an admission of being wrong can be hard to stomach. You may feel you need to do anything and everything to protect your self-esteem, and the idea of asking for forgiveness may seem out of the question.

"I Can't Live with What I Did to You!"

As uncomfortable as it might make us feel to contemplate humbling ourselves and apologizing, it's also uncomfortable to live with the guilt and shame of knowing we need to apologize but not doing so. Guilt and shame are two conditions that humans have a lot of trouble sitting with.

The two words are often used interchangeably, but in my personal experience there's a subtle difference between guilt and shame. Guilt is essentially when you know you did something wrong, or at least imagine or assume that you probably did. Shame is the pain you feel when you believe that you did something wrong, or that something about your personality or identity is wrong, whether or not you can actually identify any actual wrongdoing that you committed. I think of shame as the emotional reaction to guilt, but the two often go together; we are aware of something we did wrong, and we are ashamed at what our behavior says about who we are. "I feel so awful that I did this."

However, guilt is not always accompanied by shame. We may know we committed a wrongful act, but we don't necessarily think it means we're bad people at heart, either because the transgression was relatively small ("I forgot to return my friend's text, but I'll follow up soon") or because we don't care about the harm we caused ("Yes, I'm guilty of cheating on my taxes, but I don't feel any shame").

Guilt and shame often go hand in hand with one of our greatest fears: the fear of being exposed as bad people or caught out for our wrongdoing. We associate exposure with being criticized, ridiculed, or made to feel like an outsider. When we feel great shame, we also fear what other people may think or say about us, or how they might punish us for what we did wrong.

So of course feelings of guilt and shame can be strong motivators for wanting to seek closure. These emotions can eat at our very souls, haunt our waking hours, and keep us from getting a good night's rest.

For further illustration, here's Isabella's story. Isabella knew even before she did it that calling out her coworker Ben in an email to their boss was a crummy thing to do. She wrote a post-project email in which she grandstanded about her own contributions, then added that she was "happy to have had the opportunity to bail Ben out when he got in over his head." The truth is, Isabella has always liked working with Ben, but she is currently up for a promotion and desperate to score points. So she took a cheap shot. In her heart, Isabella knows she's guilty of nasty office politics, and she feels that what she did to Ben is unacceptable. She feels a lot of shame for her behavior and regrets her email to the boss. She wants Ben to understand why she did what she did, and to be forgiven by him. She has reached out and asked him to meet with her, but he has so far ignored her messages.

Isabella needs to resolve her own guilt and shame, and hopefully gaining Ben's forgiveness will help her do that. She also wants to continue to have a good working relationship with Ben, and she needs to heal the damage she knows she has done to his emotions so they can continue to work together productively. In other words, guilt and shame are motivating Isabella to seek closure with Ben.

SELF-ASSESSMENT: SETTING EXPECTATIONS WHEN REQUESTING FORGIVENESS

The place to begin when seeking any form of closure is self-awareness. If you feel you have harmed another person, ask yourself:

- Exactly what did I do to this person?
- How do I think, or know, it impacted them?
- Am I experiencing guilt? Shame? Both?
- Is a direct apology needed? Do I have other actions I need to take to repair the damage?
- What are the possible ways this person may react when I offer an apology? And am I prepared to cope with each of these potential responses?

"Aren't You Sorry for What You Did to Me?"

We may feel guilt and shame when we know we've wronged someone else, but we feel a different kind of discomfort when we know someone has wronged us.

If the harm is minor, our need for an apology is probably minor too. For example, if you place an online order and the wrong product arrives, forcing you to take the time to return it, you might expect an apology from this company. They apologize; you feel a sense of closure. Even if they didn't apologize, it probably wouldn't be a big deal, as long as you got your money back. People make mistakes, companies make mistakes. To demand closure for every minor transgression of daily life would be exhausting and would rob us of valuable time and energy.

But what about emotional damage that we can't simply walk away from? I'm not talking about everyday irritations like packaging errors. I mean more harmful occurrences that (hopefully) don't happen on a daily basis. Like being on the receiving end of Isabella's manipulations, as Ben was. Or discovering your partner has cheated on you when you thought you could trust them to be faithful. Or being told by a friend that a mutual friend has been saying hurtful things about you behind your back. In cases like these, an apology would be much more important. You would want and maybe even expect the other person to ask for your forgiveness.

When another person has transgressed against you in some way, real or perceived, it brings up a lot of feelings. You probably feel sad and hurt. You may also feel disappointed, because this behavior was completely contrary to your expectations for that person. How could they have done this? And don't forget anger. How dare they! (As I discussed in chapter 4, keep in mind that while anger may be a primary emotion, you may also be using your anger to cover sadness, disappointment, or other uncomfortable emotions that make you feel helpless to do anything but feel bad.)

If other people are aware of how someone else wronged you, you might have the additional pressure of feeling exposed or judged; you may fear that if you don't stand up for yourself and demand that the other person seek your forgiveness, you'll be perceived as a weak person. Returning to the example of Isabella and Ben, if their coworkers are aware of what happened between them, they may be coaching Ben on what to say to her, admonishing him not to "wimp out" and let her think what she did is okay.

Your self-esteem may also be at stake. You may wonder if you did something to deserve this kind of treatment or feel foolish for having trusted the person who hurt you. Maybe during a past conflict someone said to you, "Don't let them get away with this," and now you feel responsible for making the other person apologize, even though, of course, we can't control other people's actions. You may feel in your heart that an apology is owed to you, that this is what you need to heal your hurt feelings.

When I have conversations with clients around the desire for an apology, we frequently talk about how one person has caused great disappointment. My clients tell me stories about important people in their lives who let them down or did something that broke their trust. They talk about not being supported by someone who should have jumped in and provided an emotional rescue but instead left them stranded to fend for themselves. They talk about being attacked, usually verbally, but sometimes also physically. Clients in these situations generally describe their initial reaction as shock. Where did this come from? Why did it happen? Often, disappointment is the next response, followed by other feelings, like sadness, anger, even fear. *If this trusted person can treat me this way, what does my future look like? Can I trust anyone ever again?*

Therapists often counsel their clients not to have expectations of other people. I am certainly quick to give the mini lecture about not being able to control other people. But let's face it. When we let other people get close to us emotionally, as friends, family members, partners, or coworkers, we develop expectations of them. Why wouldn't we? To a certain extent, that's healthy. When we open ourselves up to people, we build trust, and with trust comes certain expectations. When I say this or do that, I expect and trust you not to respond in a hurtful way. We let our guards down more or less, depending on the nature of the relationship.

In many ways, the experience of having someone turn on you is a loss. You lose the version of the relationship you thought you had. And when we experience a loss, we grieve. Furthermore, a deep disappointment or betrayal can bring up feelings of past disappointments and betrayals, leaving you that much more wounded. You may be experiencing a whole accumulation of the feelings left behind by people who have hurt you in the past. The need for closure may feel all that much more urgent.

I'll give you an example. Diana had multiple sclerosis and was beginning to become symptomatic. She was having trouble walking—not a lot, but enough that her husband, Jimmy, sometimes had to take her arm. One afternoon, they arrived home after a trip to the grocery store. She was tired out, and as she got out of the car, she faltered. Jimmy quickly walked around to her side of the car and caught her arm.

Their next-door neighbor, Joyce, just happened to be in the front yard and witnessed this. She and Diana were friends, but Diana was a very private person, and she had not yet told Joyce about her diagnosis. Joyce immediately ran over to them and said, "Diana, I just saw what happened. You haven't been your old self in a long time. Please let me know how I can help." Diana explained that she had MS and asked Joyce to keep it to herself, as she didn't want to deal with answering questions from the whole neighborhood.

Joyce felt deeply saddened by this news. So saddened, in fact, that she confided in another neighbor, Brent, whom Diana was not close to. Joyce swore him to secrecy, but a couple of weeks later, Brent stopped by and offered his support to Diana. He meant well. However, Diana was horrified that word had gotten out. She felt deeply betrayed.

"I don't know if I can ever trust Joyce again," Diana told Jimmy that night. "I feel betrayed. Disappointed that she would talk behind my back. She turned me into gossip fodder. I deserved better from my friend."

"What if Joyce asked for your forgiveness?" Jimmy said. "You might feel better."

"Has she asked for forgiveness?" Diana answered. "If she has any idea what Brent did, she must know how hurt I am."

Joyce did know. Brent had bragged to her about what a sup-portive person he was and how he offered to be there for Diana, even though they weren't close. Joyce's heart sank when Brent said that. She knew what she had done. She knew Diana well enough to understand how wounded she must have felt. Can forgiveness provide some kind of closure?

SELF-ASSESSMENT: SETTING EXPECTATIONS WHEN GRANTING FORGIVENESS

If another person has apologized or is planning to apologize to you, self-awareness is once again essential. Ask yourself:

- What damage was done to me by this person?
- Am I fully aware of their level of involvement versus other factors or people who may have played a role?
- What do I need to understand for me to consider forgiveness?
- What do I need to hear from them for me to consider forgiving them? An admission of guilt? Shame? Responsibility?
- Do I want to forgive this person, or am I tempted to just use their request for forgiveness as an opportunity to inflict the pain I feel they deserve?
- What's best for me as I consider forgiving them?
- Who else is involved? What is the impact of my forgiveness, or withholding of forgiveness, on the other people who might be involved?

The Power Dynamic

You may have learned over the years, for better or worse, that human interactions often involve an exchange of power. Such a power dynamic often finds its way into attempts at closure, and most certainly when forgiveness is being given or received. One person offers an apology or asks the other person to forgive them; the other person asks for (or demands) an apology and decides whether or not to accept that apology. One person has the power to give, and one has the power to receive.

This all comes back to the ego. You know the ego. It finds its way into so many of our interactions. We want to protect our egos. Sometimes we want to protect them so much that we're willing to risk the loss of a relationship. Even if we think our ego is made of titanium, life presents us with situations in which we are faced with either admitting we have a tender spot like all humans have or putting up an impermeable wall and telling ourselves we don't care.

On one hand, the need to protect the ego can prevent us from admitting that we harmed another person. "I didn't do anything wrong. What do I care if you forgive me or not?" *My self-esteem is under attack. The ego must remain intact!* On the other hand, our egos can tell us that someone else's behavior, no matter how innocent, was somehow an affront, a deliberate act perpetrated by another person against us. "You must offer an apology! But do you even deserve my forgiveness?" *My self-esteem is under attack. The ego must remain intact!*

Offering an apology, as discussed previously in this chapter, requires acknowledging that, intentionally or unintentionally, directly or indirectly, you did something to cause harm to another person, or at least that you weren't considerate of their feelings. Essentially, offering an apology requires admitting that in some way you were wrong. This may mean having to take a look at yourself, questioning your own motives and behavior. If your self-esteem is based on satisfying the demands of the ego, including the need to always be right, this can feel threatening. An apology can be an opportunity to take a hard look at what you have built as the foundation of your self-esteem, allowing you to question whether it's built on making yourself superior to others rather than on compassion and consideration of the needs of others alongside your own. The closure you provide to the person you harmed may also give you some closure in your own life, in terms of making decisions about the person you want to be in the future. But first, you may need to decide to get beyond the demands of the ego.

Surprisingly, receiving an apology can be threatening to the ego as well, because it involves being vulnerable to the person who caused you harm. Not only are you admitting this person had the power to harm you in the first place, but also you're setting yourself up for them to refuse to admit their wrongdoing or their obligation to apologize. If that happened, then your sense of harm by this person could be doubled. This is hard to think about.

Gaining or offering forgiveness can provide needed closure when a harm has been done. But it may mean being vulnerable, taking the risk of asking what you want, admitting you were wrong. Ceding some power. That can be a tough nut for us humans to crack.

What to Expect When Forgiveness Is at Stake

As with any conversation with the goal of achieving closure, I would encourage a client who has the intention of requesting or accepting forgiveness to be clear with themselves on the potential outcomes of this conversation and whether they can accept each potential outcome. They don't necessarily need to *like* the outcome, but they have to be able to accept it. While awareness of potential outcomes does not always protect us from further emotional pain, it does help us prepare ourselves for that pain.

The ideal closure when you're seeking forgiveness looks something like this: The other person accepts your apology. You talk about what was behind the harmful behavior, why it occurred, what was intended or not intended. You decide how to move forward in your relationship. Not only does this help reduce the guilt and shame you may be feeling, it's also an opportunity to learn something about yourself, as well as your relationship.

Here are some other things to consider when seeking closure by asking for forgiveness.

- Making amends of some kind can strengthen closure. You can offer to repair the damage by, for example, contacting the other people to whom you spread a rumor about the person you're apologizing to. Or, depending on the situation, a financial remedy may be needed. Making amends shows the other person you are serious about gaining closure with them.

- An apology expressing feelings of guilt but not feelings of responsibility, or vice versa, may or may not result in forgiveness. If it seems like you're trying to assuage your own discomfort without making amends, or if it seems like you realize you committed a transgression but don't feel bad about it, the person you're apologizing to may not be satisfied and in fact may take further offense. If so, you have not achieved closure, you have deepened the wound.

- If the person you need to apologize to refuses to hear your apology, you may have to make more than one attempt to have this conversation. This may be required to show you are serious about finding closure with them. However, a word of caution: Use good judgment here. Be aware of when repeated attempts at an apology can be crossing a boundary with the other person. When it's clear that they have no desire to communicate further, stand back. You tried. They were not receptive.

- In the absence of a conversation, making amends or offering acts of kindness or service can help to bring closure or at least open the door. This may not be the closure you're hoping for, but it can be a step in the right direction.

Of course, as the person who has committed the transgression, you can ignore the whole situation and hope that the wound you caused heals on its own, that the other person forgets about it over time and your relationship gets back to normal. That isn't outside the realm of possibility. But is it what's best for your relationship? It has been my experience as a mental health professional that people often don't forget the damage other people have done to them. It gets filed away, apparently swallowed but festering nonetheless, resulting in resentment and a lack of trust that are likely to resurface in the future. Is it worth it to you to have this elephant in the room? Yes, I know that real life doesn't always look like an afterschool special on TV, but why not do what you can to create and maintain relationships built on a foundation of honesty and compassion?

Forgiveness after Death

I can say without a doubt that some of my most gut-wrenching conversations are with clients who feel they need forgiveness from a loved one who has passed away. And to be honest, anytime someone in your life passes, you probably have a few memories of times you hope the other person forgave you for the little slights we all commit against other people, the breakdowns in communication, and the blowups that are accompanied by hurt feelings.

So often, clients coping with grief will say things like "I wonder if they knew . . ." or, harder yet, "I never had a chance to . . ." In grief, we're much less likely to focus on the ways in which the person who passed caused us harm, even momentary harm, and much more likely to focus on what we did to them over the years. "Did they know how sorry I was?"

And then the hardest question of all: "How do I get closure?"

During the throes of grief, our vision of the time we spent with a loved one is not 20/20, to say the least. Our minds are focused on their death, filled with questions regarding what was said and what was not said. We desperately want to make the pain go away. Knowing we did all the right things would help diminish the pain. And if we didn't do all the right things, we want assurance that the other person forgave us. Especially if we never quite got around to asking their forgiveness or hadn't even considered the need to ask for forgiveness until it was too late.

That basic human need: to know. After death, our minds can't quite wrap themselves around what can't be known. How can we sit with the pain?

I have had clients who decided to break off contact with an elderly parent to "teach them a lesson," only to lose that parent before having the opportunity to explain why they cut them off or, all too often, to ask their forgiveness. I've had clients who had an argument with a friend and said some very unkind words to them and then lost them soon after in an accident. I've had clients, acting as caregivers for family members, who occasionally reached the limits of their patience and blew up out of emotional and physical exhaustion, and now they feel they can't live with the memories of their behavior and how their loved one reacted (or didn't react). They have come to me after the fact to help them sort through their fragmented emotions. Unrelenting grief. Begging for forgiveness, for absolution, for some kind of closure.

We can't gain forgiveness from someone who has passed. Stumbling upon a letter they left for us granting us closure pretty much only happens in the movies. We can't ask for their forgiveness, not now. It's too late. Therefore, I encourage my clients to focus on the big picture of their relationship, when they're ready to do that. This helps them allow themselves to be human, to accept that they did the best they could with the knowledge and the resources they had at the time. To focus not on what they didn't do and what they regret, but rather on the times when they tried to be there for their loved one, when they tried to support them in the ways they knew how. In the dynamics of any relationship there are arguments and unkind words, but there are also moments of happiness and connection.

Sometimes I am successful in helping clients have a balanced view of their time with the person they lost, to see the ebbs and flows of human relationships, to embrace the big picture, their own human gifts and flaws as well as those of the person they lost. Sometimes I am not so successful, and they are only able to see their transgressions against this person. Guess what? Sometimes that's what the relationship was mostly about, and they are left with their guilt and shame, shouting at God or the universe about the unfairness of life, begging for one more chance at closure.

Closure is not only about having heart-to-heart conversations, which is especially important to consider when someone has passed. Closure can also be about choosing to do better. Living as the person who passed would have liked us to live. Embodying the values they would have liked to see us embody. Doing acts of kindness in their name.

Sometimes we have to get creative about finding closure. Searching your own heart for ways to achieve closure may be an important step toward healing yourself.

EXERCISE:
FORGIVING AND BEING FORGIVEN

Forgiveness often comes in the form of written words: a letter, a text, an email. Look back into your past. Identify a person who harmed you in some way, as a child or as an adult, and write the letter that you would like to receive from them asking for your forgiveness. Then identify a person you have harmed over the years and write a letter of apology to them. These letters aren't meant to be shared; they are only for you. After you write them, savor the satisfaction that comes from forgiving and being forgiven. Getting your thoughts down on paper (or on the screen) can be deeply satisfying. And consider: this may go a long way toward providing the closure you really need, even without the participation of the other people involved.

Closing Thought:
It's Still Worth Considering

Us poor humans. We're out there bouncing off each other like a steel pinball being shot through a pinball machine. Sometimes we act out of our best instincts and create connection, goodwill, mutual benefit, loving kindness. Sometimes we don't and create damage to whomever happened to be there at the time, often to those we love the most. We sure can be mean to each other. Then we're left picking up the pieces of our own troubled hearts, the damage we caused, the damage we sustained. We need to ask for forgiveness, but our pride gets in the way. We need to forgive, but our pride gets in the way.

Sometimes the potential for humans to forgive and to accept forgiveness is realized. Closure occurs. It can feel like a miracle. And it kind of is. Closure through forgiveness is not always possible for all kinds of reasons. It's still worth considering. Maybe even attempting.

Chapter 7

It's Part of a Cycle

Often when we think of closure, a one-time event is the first thing that comes to mind. Something happened that left us wanting resolution, whether it was as small as getting cut off in traffic or as large as losing a loved one. These are the kinds of events we've primarily focused on in the previous four chapters about wanting closure because we're hurting, we're angry, we feel helpless, or we need forgiveness. But perhaps the most common reason we want closure is as part of a cycle that plays out over and over in our everyday lives.

Humans have a way of falling into behavioral patterns. We seem to be wired that way. We do it on our own and with each other too. These patterns can provide a sense of security and trust because they let us know what we can expect from each other. But they can also be destructive, because so many patterns revolve around doing damage to each other, followed by gaining closure in some form to tie up all those dangling loose ends and heal the pain . . . only to fall back into another repetition of the same cycle.

Sound familiar? If so, let me start with some reassurance: you sure aren't alone.

Somewhat paradoxically, insisting on closure can be all about *not* getting closure. Here's what I mean. If you don't get the closure you wanted or thought you needed, you may be tempted to try again. If you feel the other person got closure but you didn't, you may be tempted to try again. This makes sense, but it's also potentially a trap. It means not only that a given situation may never be resolved but also that the people involved will never accept a lack of closure and move on either. One or both of them will continue making attempts at closure, with varying levels of success. The relationship swings between being relatively happy and stable and being relatively unhappy and unstable, depending on where they are in this cycle. "And the beat goes on," as the classic Sonny and Cher tune goes.

This cycle occurs often in codependent relationships, in which one person is a caregiver and the other is a taker. The caregiver may seek closure, hoping the other person will finally admit how much has been done for them, how much they love, need, and appreciate the eternally giving caretaker. *When are you finally going to admit how much you need me? Or finally release me so I can get a life?* But the imbalance continues, and the caregiver is left still wanting closure.

This pattern can also occur in a relationship that is just plain toxic. Take, for example, two people who treat each other horribly, both knowing deep in their hearts that they would be better off in a healthier relationship or even alone, but they can't quite rip the bandage off and move on. They have that closure talk, again. They agree to move on, again—until a few days later when they find another reason to come back together, again. It's reminiscent of another classic tune: "Break Up to Make Up" by the Stylistics. When a toxic relationship involves verbal or physical abuse, it is especially tragic to see two people caught in a cycle of pain that they both know needs to end.

But unhealthy dynamics like codependence, toxicity, and abuse are not the only causes of this cycle. Most of us fall into this pattern at one time or another. It can happen in romantic relationships, in the workplace, with family members, and elsewhere, as we'll explore in this chapter.

Stuck in a Love-Hate Relationship

Romantic relationships are uncomplicated only in our dreams. In real life, they're messy. Sometimes they're so messy we have to ask ourselves what keeps us there—that is, if we're honest enough to answer that question. Have you ever been in a relationship that seemed to have so much potential but you were never able to quite reach that potential? Instead, you'd have times of connectedness alternating with times when you seemed to be on different planets, not communicating (and maybe even outright abusing each other).

But you stuck around. You talked things out, you made promises to each other, you got closure, and you were ready to move forward. But you fell back into the old patterns. Or you decided the only closure was to end things. And so you did. But then you found your way back to each other.

Relationships can be addictive. We get addicted to the endorphin rush of being around the other person, especially when a relationship is in its early stages, but we also get addicted to the rush of righteous anger we feel during arguments. We get hooked on feeling sad and attracting sympathy for the suffering we endure. Closure provides a rush of its own, and we can get addicted to that as well.

This is a familiar relationship pattern among the clients I encounter in my work. I find this dynamic often occurs when you're early in the relationship game, still learning what you want and don't want in a relationship, still deciding what you will and won't put up with in a partner. But I have also had clients who have spent many years in one relationship after another repeating this same pattern, using a desire for closure as a reason to avoid ending a relationship, keeping each other stuck in an endless cycle of unhappiness. And most tragically, I have seen couples continue this pattern for years.

Like Nick and Emma. Nick and Emma have been together for years. They've talked about marriage from time to time, but they never move forward with it. Why? Because for them, "together" is loosely defined. Sure, they have all the outward signs of a solid relationship. Their parents know each other, their friends know each other, even their coworkers know each other. They have a great apartment and enjoy inviting friends over for meals. So what's wrong with this picture? Well, a lot.

Nick and Emma have had a lot of ups and downs over the years, periods of not speaking followed by periods of being back in each other's company. Over what, you might wonder? They just don't seem to be able to get along for very long between breakdowns. They disagree over simple things like who does what chores. After living together for a few years, they still don't have a rhythm in place to keep their home running. They argue about spending money, most recently in public while shopping—not an infrequent occurrence. They disagree on vacations, on politics . . . you name the issue, they're probably at odds. Both of them often make a joke to their closest friends when the other one isn't present about how they can't live with each other and can't live without each other.

So what happens to keep them together? You guessed it. The cycle of seeking closure. They sit down together and lay it all out on the table, sometimes with angry words and accusations. They promise each other to do better. They reaffirm their desire to stay together, maybe with some great makeup sex to seal the deal. Or alternatively they agree that it's time to call it quits. They retreat to separate areas of the apartment and both start looking for other living arrangements. But they never quite find their way to pulling the plug. Sooner than later, they kiss and make up—and start making each other miserable again.

Everything seems fine for a couple of weeks. It's not clear if the cycle begins or ends with closure, but it's safe to say that whatever they agreed upon, or agreed to disagree about, soon becomes a reason for another argument.

If you've been in a similar relationship, you can probably relate. You might even have cringed a few times as you read their story. The truth of the matter is that as much as they might state otherwise, Nick and Emma aren't in a compatible relationship. In fact, their relationship probably qualifies as toxic. They seem to exist to make each other unhappy. They come together temporarily for closure, but it only serves to perpetuate another unhappy cycle. If they were seeking closure in a productive way, it could be a means of freeing each other to get on with their lives, or of creating the foundation for closing the door on the past and opening the door to a new, more functional version of their relationship. But for Nick and Emma, closure is a means of finding excuses to stay in an unhappy union.

EXERCISE: CREATE A TIMELINE

Think about the relationship you're currently in or a relationship from your recent past. Take a sheet of paper and create a timeline mapping out the highs and lows of your relationship. What were the major events along the way? What emotions did you experience? Are there upward trends? Downward trends? What caused the ups and downs? At what points along the way in your relationship did you seek closure? For what reason? And what was the outcome? Did you achieve closure? What followed?

This may be a painful process. You might feel exposed to yourself. But it's a great way to identify for yourself what has worked in your relationship and what has caused you pain. You might learn something about yourself in the process, including what you want to work on for yourself or what you want to avoid in your next relationship.

Stuck in a Love-Hate Job

Have you ever been in a job where, in your heart of hearts, you weren't quite sure what kept you there? Where you had every reason to stay, but you also seemed to have every reason to leave? Maybe you talked to your boss and expressed your frustration. Promises were made. You stayed, hoping for the best. But the promises weren't kept. Maybe you even had that final conversation after getting an offer elsewhere. You told your boss you were through with the whole place. But they talked you into staying, giving you a little more money and promising things would get better. You stayed because you just *knew* it would get better now that they knew you *could* leave if they didn't keep their promises. They still didn't.

Stewart had been working at a boutique ad agency for three years. It was owned by Lori, who hired Stewart during the first year of operation. Stewart often describes his job to his friends as "emotional boot camp." Between the difficult and sometimes abusive clients, the salary that's lower than he could make at another agency, and the long hours, he had days and weeks when he wasn't sure how much longer he could do it. But he continued. He joked that while he liked working at a so-called hot agency, he wished all that hotness could be used to pay his rent.

What kept him there? Lori promised him a big bonus at the end of the year. And a raise. But when the end of the year came around, she explained that the bonus wasn't going to be possible after all. She gave him a raise, but it was smaller than he expected. Stewart told her how used he felt and said he was going to start job hunting. Lori expressed to him how valuable he was to the company and how sad it would be to see him leave, but she didn't try to convince him to stay.

After this conversation, Stewart felt like he had some closure. After all, he'd vented his frustration, which he had needed to do for a long time, and he'd received acknowledgment of his value to the agency. He felt ready to find a new job. Finally. Big sigh of relief.

A couple of days later, however, Lori asked Stewart to meet with her. She attempted to dissuade him from leaving. She promised that at the end of the next year he would be, in her words, "made whole"—provided with the compensation he had been promised. A double bonus and a bigger raise, to make up for what he hadn't received this year.

Once again, the end of the year came around. Lori gave Stewart the bonus she'd promised him the year before but not the additional one for this year. He also got a cost-of-living raise but nothing more. Lori informed him that due to a couple of lost accounts, that was the best she could do. But she promised that he would receive this year's bonus and another one at the end of the next year. Lori again said she had every intention of "making Stewart whole." He just needed to be patient one more year. Stewart expressed his frustration and came just short of calling her a liar.

Maybe this *was the closure I really needed*, he told himself later. *I'm* really *ready to move on this time*. But he couldn't bring himself to quit. He wanted to prove to himself and to Lori that he could be a success at this hot company. He thought about what that double bonus would come to, how the company needed to keep their promises and treat him with the respect he deserved as a dedicated employee. He decided that that was the closure he really needed—not more words but a fat check. And so he stayed.

What's going on here? Lori and Stewart are caught in a cycle. Stewart threatens to walk, Lori says she understands why. Lori promises to reward him for all his hard work, and Stewart wants to believe her and achieve the happy ending he feels he deserves. Stewart can't quite close the door behind him, and Lori can't help finding a way to keep it open. They need each other to act out this drama.

In the workplace, we often equate money with love. When our job withholds money from us, it results in feelings that are less about the money itself and more about our value as human beings. Aside from the basic need to pay our bills, that's what keeps us stuck in cycles of frustration, exploitation, or even abuse like what Stewart experienced (and yes, for Stewart, I suspect there's a story from childhood as well). And it's why closure can feel so necessary.

I frequently have conversations with clients who are at the end of their patience with their jobs, for similar reasons to Stewart's. But when a boss like Lori dangles more dollars in front of them, they take the bait. They stick around for what they think would be the ultimate closure: the money, the promotion, the recognition they're owed. Validation. Vindication. And so they head into round two of seeking closure. Or round three, or four. It's hard to leave when you feel tortured with business that always seems to stay unfinished. We allow ourselves to be strung along, waiting for the ultimate closure that will finally allow us, as Lori said so persuasively, to be "made whole."

It's important, I think, to keep in mind that work relationships can push our love button, so to speak. We may not approach these relationships in the same ways or for the same reasons as we would approach relationships with friends, romantic partners, or family members, but as humans, we don't usually treat them as "just business" either. Even if the work relationships aren't particularly intense in and of themselves, they can be powerful reminders of other relationships; if we always struggled to win our parents' approval, for example, we might subconsciously struggle to win our bosses' approval as well. As a result, the need for closure is intensified and we're also more likely to stick around in an unsatisfactory or toxic situation, hoping we finally get the closure we feel we deserve.

Just Can't Stop Dancing That Family Dance

I can't discuss closure that is essentially an excuse not to let go without talking about families. You may be totally cringing at this point, and I haven't even gotten started. All families have their dysfunctionality, at least all the families I've come into contact with. So again, let me assure you that if you have some dysfunctional behaviors in your family, not only are you not alone—you're normal.

When I discuss family dysfunction with my clients, I use the term *family dance*. Somebody turns on the metaphorical music, a favorite tune, and everybody gets up and does the family dance. Examples of family dances are ongoing tension between a parent and a child, competition between siblings, or a parent who is needy on one hand or abusive on the other. Family dances are especially obvious during get-togethers like around the holidays, but most likely they go on all year long. And closure? Closure in these situations comes in many forms. A big family blowup. A conversation with lots of airing of grievances, followed by promises that may or may not be kept. Periods of not speaking, grudge marathons, followed by a gradual warming up.

Closure is part of the family dance. Closure is part of the

drama, a door that is shut and then soon opened. The music keeps playing. Everybody keeps dancing.

Eva has always had a very difficult relationship with her mother, Marta, tension that Marta has never had with Eva's brother, José. Eva often jokes to José that she should never have been born, or at least not born female. Marta has also been known to joke to José that boys are a lot easier to raise than girls. Marta never seems to be happy with anything Eva does. She second-guesses her hairstyles, her clothing, what she does for a living, the men she dates. Marta has been critical of Eva for as long as Eva can remember—and Eva is now in her early thirties. Eva and José's father seems to know how to stay clear of the tension between his wife and daughter, but José hasn't figured out how to do that.

The tension between Eva and Marta simmers for months at a time until it boils over. It doesn't take much for that to happen. Another barbed comment from Marta, a perceived slight from Eva, and the fight is on. An argument, followed by the silent treatment. When they go silent, that's when José is brought into the game, and the triangle is resurrected. Marta calls her son to complain about what Eva did to hurt her feelings or about a decision Eva has made that she doesn't agree with. Soon after, Eva calls to complain about what her mother did to make her feel bad about herself this time.

And how does José respond? He acts as the peacemaker. He soothes his mother's feelings, then soothes his sister's feelings. He provides his perspective to Eva on what set their mother off and then he does the same for Marta. He encourages them to get together, generally advising each of them to act as if nothing happened. He might even invite them over to his own house to act as mediator in person.

Marta and Eva have a good laugh together and resolve to try to get along better. After all, aren't they mother and daughter?

They both agree that they see the other person's perspective. Closure. José is emotionally exhausted but glad they've reached a truce. Until the next time.

Sound familiar? Every family I have ever known has a family dance. On the surface it may seem healthy, and not all family dances are about dysfunctionality. Family dances might include teaming up to provide lots of encouragement to a sibling who suffers from low self-esteem; a way of joking that is almost a secret language all the family members share; or supportive competition among siblings that helps to continually push them all toward more excellence.

However, family dances can also be all about perpetuating dysfunctionality. Have you experienced that in your family? And if so, have you also observed that the family dance includes repeated attempts at closure that provide temporary relief but also open the door to the next cycle?

Some of the best and worst examples of this cycle that I have experienced in my work are the family dances that keep the family member with an addiction or mental illness from getting the help they need. This tends to happen because the other family members subconsciously need the addicted or mentally ill person to be the focus of their frustrations, the reason for the family's problems, and an excuse not to look at their own issues. Behind this person's back, family members may lament about how troubled they are, criticize them for being weak, and complain about the energy and attention they require. Closure comes in the form of trips to rehab or promises to adhere to medication and therapy regimens, followed by a round of hugs and tears. But this is only temporary closure. The other family members enable the member with the addiction or mental illness to fall apart again, because they need them to be the loser.

And the beat goes on. That is, until someone refuses to dance.

The Devil You Know

You have probably heard the expression "Better the devil you know than the one you don't." Humans are hardwired for consistency. We don't like change; even positive changes that we have actively chosen, like a new job or a new home; change causes us to feel stress. We dislike change so much that we can easily allow ourselves to become stuck in our familiar zone, even if that familiar zone is unpleasant or downright destructive. Staying with the devil you know is a way of avoiding the uncertainty that accompanies change. Even when we're in a bad situation that makes us deeply unhappy, we can talk ourselves into sticking it out because at least we know what to expect. There is no uncertainty when we know each day will be as painful as the day before: The toxic work situation that is at least predictable. The bad relationship that feels less scary than being out on the dating scene again. The family dances that we endure because, after all, that's what families do.

Seeking closure can lead to freedom. But it can also be used to delude ourselves into thinking that the situation is going to have a happy ending, that we are finally taking the necessary steps to improve a toxic situation or to extract promises from the other person that will make everything better. In these cases, closure doesn't do its job, because deep down we don't want it to. We're not ready. We fear the uncertainty—or the emptiness—that we might be left with when the pain is taken away.

And making up is just so much fun and so deeply satisfying. For a while.

Particularly in a romantic relationship between two people who are making each other unhappy but can't seem to either repair their relationship or end it, the quest for closure can take various routes, but they all end with the same destination: the next round of discussions about closure. These discussions are often very emotional, with lots of yelling or crying. All that emotion is part of the glue that keeps the couple stuck together. Lots of emotions, lots of promises. But most likely not a lot of action or change.

Why? Because in their heart of hearts, neither person really wants change. If you've been in a relationship like this, you know what I mean. The way you treat each other is so ingrained, so familiar, that you soon find yourself slipping back into the old familiar pattern. Sure, you'll get fed up over time, and you'll seek closure. And you'll get closure—that closure that is as much a part of the fabric of your relationship as is the unhappiness that inevitably follows.

The Myth of Perfect Equity in Relationships

"Let's sit down and talk about what I'm giving and what you're giving, what I should get and what you should get. If we can finally even the playing field, then I can rest a lot easier. I'll have closure." This sentiment can all too often be the beginning of a series of conversations around closure. Why a series? Because if the focus of your relationship is to make sure that you and your partner are both contributing exactly the same amount to the relationship at all times, you are going to have a lot of these conversations. Over and over.

These feelings of inequity start early. If you grew up with siblings, you probably have memories of having to share, whether it was household tasks, the last cupcake, or getting to sit in the front seat on the way to the grocery store. You might also have had to share the attention of your parents or other caretakers, and you may sometimes—or often—have felt like you didn't get as much attention from them as your siblings did. ("Mom always liked you better.") When children feel they're not getting what their siblings are getting, whether it's unequal attention to physical or emotional needs on one hand, or excessive criticism or punishment on the other, this can lead to very primal feelings of deprivation. On the other end of the spectrum, children who grow up without siblings may have unrealistic expectations of what they should be receiving or confusion about what it means to share, because they don't usually have to share with anyone.

In school, feelings of unfairness and inequity are most likely intensified, regardless of experiences at home. A teacher may seem to treat some kids better than others. Not everybody gets picked to be on the sports team or in the school play, even if those who were not chosen feel they were just as talented or worked just as hard as those who were. In the education system, we move from one inequitable situation to the next. Sometimes we win, sometimes we lose. Maybe a lot of the time we lose. "It's not fair." "They got more than me." That achy sense of loose ends can have an impact on self-esteem and self-confidence.

And it can resurface in our romantic relationships as adults. When I speak with couples, the issue of equity invariably comes up. Who's bringing in the most money, and what do they feel that entitles them to? Who's doing more of the household chores, and what led to this division of labor? Who's taking more responsibility for the kids? These are only a few of the areas in which couples commonly feel that their relationship is unbalanced in some way. "When are you going to understand that I'm the one doing all the work, and to start doing your share? I'm investing in the relationship, and what am I getting back?"

Unfortunately, feelings of inequity in a relationship can lead to the demise of the relationship if they're not addressed. Attaining closure in a situation like this ideally provides emotional satisfaction—not necessarily complete emotional satisfaction, but at least some. In the case of inequity, this satisfaction may range from attaining some recognition that one party was being treated unfairly, to reparations of some kind with a blueprint for a way forward. This process can be complicated, requiring both individuals to lower their defenses and listen to each other, and to be willing to accept their share of responsibility and change their behavior. Without that level of openness, closure is temporary, leaving the door open to more conflict around inequity and more attempts to seek more temporary closure.

On the other hand, insisting on precise equality of contribution in a romantic relationship can be just as deadly to a relationship. Why? Because it is only human nature, when you feel you are giving more than you are getting, to begin to feel resentment. Resentment can lead one partner to withhold from the other partner, passive-aggressively refusing to help around the house, waiting for it to get messy enough that their partner finally figures out what they aren't doing and pitches in. It might mean refusing to make social plans out of a belief that the other partner is skating by and letting their partner be the social director. Withholding can also lead to refusing intimacy.

What's happening here? One partner has decided to keep score. And they've decided they've accumulated many points. They feel that because they're contributing so much more than their partner, they're the "winner" in the relationship. And shouldn't the winner be rewarded in some way? What's the prize? And in the absence of a prize, should the other partner be punished in some way? Again, this leads to the potential for more withholding behavior.

I want to clarify that it is not my intention to minimize what's involved in navigating the difficult process of determining what is equitable in a relationship, whether it's a relationship between romantic partners, friends, family members, or members of an organization or community. This can be a complicated process that, of course, involves much more than the intervention of a therapist (though I have to say that mental health professionals could sure play a useful role in these situations!). If a relationship is consistently and unfairly one-sided, the emotional impact of inequity can be debilitating.

But even the strongest relationships have ebbs and flows. Sometimes your partner needs more support; other times you need more support. You also contribute to the relationship in different ways. Your partner may be better at planning; you may be better at implementing. The point here is that scorekeeping doesn't work, because it's impossible to quantify what each of you brings to your relationship. I have this discussion often with couples in which one partner has a chronic condition, requiring a lot of household, financial, and emotional support. In this situation, the ebbs might last a whole lot longer than the flows. Sometimes being in a relationship means dropping everything to be there for your partner; as we get older, the chances of this increase.

What does this have to do with closure? We may think we're seeking closure on an issue when actually we're being withholding or passive-aggressive. "If I force us to contribute evenly, then I won't have to feel this resentment all the time." "I will stop doing this until you pick up the slack." "You will finally appreciate me, and you will look for ways to contribute more to the relationship and make me happier."

I can say with certainty that this is not the way to achieve closure when you feel your partner is not bringing as much to the relationship as you are. Instead, it will likely do more damage to your relationship, because your partner will begin to find their own ways to withhold in a competition to make the biggest and harshest point.

A Few Words of Concern

There is no shame in being stuck in a relationship in which closure is not really closure but a door to more unhappiness. It's human. If you were sitting with me in my office, you would only feel compassion coming from me, not judgment. However, as I often say to my clients, you ultimately have a choice as to whether you want to stay stuck in a potentially destructive rut or move on with your life.

Let me ask you a harder question: Does this keep happening to you? Being in one relationship that is causing you distress but that you just can't break free of is one thing. Having a history of being caught in multiple relationships like this is another. This is an emotionally destructive pattern that leaves you in a constant state of feeling diminished, disempowered, and depleted. It may be a sign of codependence, a mental illness, or a personality disorder—all conditions that are treatable, but not through a book alone. A mental health professional can talk to you about emotionally destructive relationship patterns, help you identify what's attracting you to the people or situations you find yourself involved with, and work with you on making changes. So if you find yourself in the cycle of fruitlessly seeking closure in one relationship after another, it may be time to get some help. Don't go through this alone.

And I just have to add one more concern. The "I just can't quit you" relationships that I discussed in this chapter may also include domestic violence, or, as we now call it, intimate partner violence. IPV doesn't involve only physical abuse; it can involve psychological abuse, legal abuse, social media abuse, financial abuse, and other forms of abuse. One of the most heartbreaking aspects of my work as a mental health professional is working with clients experiencing IPV. All too often, IPV includes a pattern of periods of abuse, leading up to seeking closure with lots of tears and promises of doing better, or gaslighting and victim-blaming followed by more abuse. This abuse can increase in intensity and danger over time, with each round of false closure opening the door to an intensification of the abuse. If you feel that you may be experiencing IPV in your relationship, with closure that leads only to more abuse, it's time to reach out for help.

SELF-ASSESSMENT:
THE CLOSURE CYCLE

In this chapter, I've discussed relationships in which seeking closure perpetuates a cycle of dysfunction. If you're caught in a relationship like this and are looking to find closure, here are some questions to ask yourself. These are hard questions, but the answers are worthwhile.

- When was the last time we sought closure? What was the issue we were discussing?
- Looking back, was the goal of achieving closure on that issue realistic? Achievable?
- How did we do in achieving that goal? Was the closure we found complete? Incomplete?
- How did I feel after seeking closure? Mad? Sad? Glad? Afraid?
- What happened in our relationship after we attempted to achieve closure?
- How long before we slid back into the day-to-day pattern?
- And the hardest question of all: What's keeping us together? What's in it for me?

Closing Thought:
Not All Relationships Are Meant to Be

I am all about looking for the silver lining in the dark clouds, identifying what's possible, working to make relationships work. Having said that, I have worked with many, many clients stuck in destructive relationships—romantic relationships, work relationships, family relationships, and friendships. I have worked with them to find closure in a way that might lead to positive change, and I do believe people are capable of change.

However, my clients in situations like the ones I have discussed in this chapter are often in relationships with people who have agendas, such that they need the other person to think or behave in a certain way to achieve their agenda. And I have had clients who were so beaten down, disempowered, or caught in the cycle of trying to prove themselves worthy that they didn't realize their repeated attempts to get closure, love, or respect were a form of false hope.

So what is the role of closure in a relationship that is based on a pattern of destructive behavior? Sometimes the best closure is to accept that there is no closure. This is the acceptance I talked about in chapter 2 and will talk about more in part 4 of this book. Sometimes you have to accept you will never get what you want from that person and you will never know why. And then, depending on the relationship, you walk away.

The sad truth is that not all relationships work. Sometimes a relationship declines into button-pushing, manipulation, withholding, and other destructive behavior. Closure can mend a relationship, or at least provide an opportunity to agree to disagree and end the cycle of mutual destruction. But closure can also provide false hope, opening the door to further dysfunction or abuse. Being a mentally healthy person can require you to ask yourself some difficult questions, be willing to take a hard look at yourself, and take the risks required to find your own happiness.

Part III
How to Seek Closure

Chapter 8

Set Your Intentions

n part 1, we defined what closure is and is not, and in part 2
we explored in-depth our reasons for wanting closure—some
healthy, some not so healthy, but all very human. In part 3, we'll
bring our new understanding into the real world and discuss the
concrete steps we can take to seek closure in productive and mean-
ingful ways. That starts with intentionality.

You probably noticed that part 2 included exercises and self-
assessment questions throughout each chapter. The purpose of
these activities is to help you take a closer look at the thoughts
and feelings behind your desire to seek closure. In this chapter,
you'll dig deeper with more questions and exercises to help you
clarify your intentions and determine the best approach to seek-
ing closure (if indeed you decide to move forward with seeking
closure at all). The goal here is to help you approach closure from
a position of strength and empowerment, so that you don't act out
of desperation or anger and ultimately cause even more harm to
yourself or someone else. When you act with intentionality, you
have the best chance of achieving closure in a way that genuinely
helps you—and of recognizing when closure is impossible and

choosing to walk away. Let's dive in and learn about setting Inten-
tions.

The Importance of Intention

Initially, when you want closure, you just *want it*. As soon as pos-
sible. Right now. The anger, the sadness, the fear, the frustration . . .
It's all been building up, and it's uncomfortable, and it has to be
released. You just want to feel better, and you believe only getting
closure will make all these bad feelings go away.

And so you don't think. You just act.

And then, afterward, when you don't get the results you were
hoping for, you realize that when it really came down to it, you
weren't all that clear on *why* you needed closure. You hadn't thought
through the best way to present your case. You hadn't considered
how the other person might react to your request (or demand).
You were seeking closure from a place of reactivity and panic, not
a position of clarity and strength.

You lacked, in a word, intentionality.

In mental health, we talk a lot about intentionality these days.
We teach our clients why it's important to be clear on our inten-
tions in day-to-day situations. We help them understand their in-
tentions as they approach an interaction with another person, then
we communicate those intentions to that person in a way they can
hear and understand. And we guide them to recognize when cer-
tain intentions mean that it's not in their best interest to pursue a
certain course of action, including one that might lead to achiev-
ing closure.

In a nutshell, intentionality means:

- Understanding the motives behind your desire to
  communicate

- Being aware of what you hope to accomplish in your communication
- Knowing what you want to say and how you want to say it
- Having realistic expectations regarding how the other person may react

In terms of closure, this means asking yourself:

- Why do I need closure in this situation?
- What am I hoping to accomplish by talking with this person?
- What is the best way to approach this conversation?
- Given what I know about and have experienced with this person, what are realistic possible outcomes?

Becoming fully aware of your own intentionality may not be a comfortable process. It requires asking yourself some hard questions, looking deep inside yourself, and evaluating your experiences. Yes, you'll think about how the other person contributed to whatever situation you're in, but you'll look at your own role as well. Getting clear with yourself on how you may have contributed to the situation isn't easy; in fact, it can be downright hard. But when you do the work that enables you to act with intentionality, the results can be powerful.

Why? Because this work lets you arrive at a place where you're fully engaging your rational mind instead of getting caught up in the emotions of the moment. When we feel we're being treated unfairly, an emotional response is triggered. Similarly, when we feel we have wronged someone else, an emotional response is triggered. Let's be honest—just about any interaction with another human being can trigger an emotional response. And when we feel bad in some way, we want to do something to make ourselves feel better.

That need to feel better is a fundamental reason for seeking closure. But successful closure requires getting past the immediate emotional reaction so that you can act in a way that directly addresses the situation. So that the adults involved can have an adult discussion. Now, I'm all about acknowledging your feelings, feeling your feelings, honoring your feelings. But the way we *act* on those feelings is just as important. And if we don't engage our rational mind in addition to feeling our feelings, we can end up acting in a way that is unproductive or harmful to ourselves and to other people.

Sure, emotions may come up in the process of seeking closure, even very strong emotions. But intentionality can help ensure that the emotions don't become so overpowering that you lose sight of what you're trying to achieve, damaging a relationship further and feeling even more disempowered in the process. As we all know, actions have consequences; the rational mind helps protect us from unexpected and unwanted consequences.

Examining Your Emotions

If you didn't have a lot of emotions around what happened between you and the person with whom you're seeking closure, you wouldn't be seeking closure in the first place. Taking the time to sort through and identify the specifics of these emotions is an important aspect of intentionality. It not only helps you gain clarity for yourself but also lets you prepare yourself better for the closure conversation.

For example, you don't want to rush into action if you're feeling intense sadness. It's much better to be aware of these feelings, to look at the source of your sadness, to talk about it with an objective person, and to have some perspective on your sadness. Other feelings may come up for you, including anger, frustration, or fear. I encourage you to examine all these feelings, to bring them into the light of day, to understand them, and to take ownership of them.

In a difficult conversation, lots of emotional buttons can be pushed. If you haven't really taken the time to examine your feelings, you may suddenly find yourself overwhelmed by feelings you had not before acknowledged and dealt with. This can potentially result in a conversation that doesn't go anywhere, because you're so overwhelmed that you're unable to address the issues at hand. And to be honest, being emotionally overwhelmed can place you in the position of being manipulated or gaslighted by the person you're trying to find closure with, putting you right back in the same dynamic that created the need for closure in the first place. By the same token, it can affect your own actions, resulting in words or behaviors that create harm to the other person and/or your relationship.

Mindfulness can be a useful technique for identifying feelings. Take time to sit with yourself in a quiet place. Do some calming breathing. Visualize past interactions with this person that have brought you to this point. As you visualize these interactions, also do some journaling. Write the thoughts that come up about yourself, your relationship, and any associated feelings. This will help you to identify the feelings that are bubbling up. Some may be especially strong. These are the feelings that I encourage you to take a closer look at, to understand where they're coming from, to talk through before you seek closure. If you don't feel you're able to approach closure from this perspective, then initiating a conversation about it is not likely to benefit you or the person you're seeking closure from.

Clarifying Your Communication

Acting intentionally is a two-step process. First, you do the hard work of clarifying your intentions for yourself rather than immediately reacting to your emotions in a way you'll regret later. And then, once you've achieved that inner clarity, you use it to effectively communicate your feelings and thoughts to the person with whom you're seeking closure. If you haven't taken the time to look deep inside yourself and understand your intentions in seeking closure, you won't be in a good position to convey them to the other person—how could you be?—and the conversation can easily be derailed. But if you do understand your intentions, you're in a better position to communicate why you think and feel as you do, describe what kind of closure you're seeking, and clarify what you do and don't intend in a way that's more likely to lead to understanding.

As I have said previously, we don't have control over how other people think, feel, or behave. However, when you speak with intentionality, there's a better chance the other person will be able to listen without getting defensive, because you're speaking honestly from the "I" and taking ownership of your own feelings, rather than speaking from the more accusatory-sounding "you." Intentionality means speaking from the heart with honesty, respect, and compassion. It helps you avoid damaging a relationship by causing the other person to feel unfairly attacked or blamed. It also helps you avoid exacerbating your own suffering by asking for something that you've come to realize the other person can't or won't give you. That's a powerful foundation for a conversation about closure.

Here's an example of intentionality in action.

Beth and Fernanda have been in a relationship for a few years. Fernanda grew up in a very stable family, but Beth did not. Beth continues to be very involved with her family, contributing financially to her parents monthly, which has an impact on the couple's financial situation. While Fernanda has worked to be under-standing, Beth's family takes up a lot of Beth's income and time, including frequent weekend visits to her parents in another state. Fernanda feels like Beth has prioritized her family over their rela-tionship, and that Beth has become so involved with solving her parents' problems that she isn't committed to their relationship any longer.

Fernanda has talked with Beth about her feelings. They even had a few sessions of couples counseling. But she doesn't see any change. Fernanda feels sad but also angry. If she's honest with her-self, she feels mostly angry. She doesn't see any progress; in fact, Beth is spending more and more time with her parents and has also become involved in caring for a sibling with a substance abuse problem, which has left her further preoccupied with family mat-ters. Fernanda has tried to help, tried to be emotionally support-ive, but Beth has put a wall up between them, saying things like "I can handle this on my own."

Fernanda knows in her heart that this situation is not going to change and that she needs to have the big breakup conversation with Beth. But when she starts to formulate how to say what she wants Beth to hear and understand, she mostly gets back in touch with her anger. Then she starts thinking about how she feels she deserves to blow up at Beth, to unleash all her pent-up anger, her hurt feelings, her disappointment, her fears about a future with-out Beth. That might feel good in the moment, but it sure wouldn't give Beth or Fernanda the closure Fernanda thinks they both need if they're going to move on from each other. Fernanda knows this wouldn't be productive, that it would only result in more pain, not closure.

Fernanda takes some time to get clear with herself on her in-tentions regarding finding closure with Beth so that she can talk to her about the reasons for her disappointment and anger, rather than just dumping her anger all over her. In doing so, Fernanda gets clear with herself that she wants Beth to know how much she has meant to her, why the relationship ceased to work, and how they can find a path to ending their relationship equitably and with mutual compassion. Fernanda knows Beth well enough to know that she will listen to a rational discussion if she has the opportunity to respond and tell her side, but would walk away if Fernanda tried to unleash her rage. (Again, that would not achieve closure anyway.) Fernanda is also clear in her mind that she intends to listen to Beth, to hear her side.

Fernanda takes some time to sort through her feelings, starting with allowing herself to really feel her feelings, including her anger. Then she steps back from her feelings and uses her rational mind to consider the history of their relationship—what brought them together, the great times they've shared—as well as her own needs and expectations. She defines her intention as first and foremost to treat Beth with love and compassion.

When she eventually initiates the conversation, she says to Beth, "I love you so much, but I think we're at different places in our relationship. I respect what you're doing for your family, but I don't feel like our relationship is important to you anymore. I can't continue to live this way."

"I agree," Beth says. "We are at different places. And right now my place is with my family. I don't expect you to understand this. But I hope you can accept that this is what I need to do."

Beth and Fernanda wish each other well and thank each other for the good times they shared. They both feel sad to be parting ways but comforted to know their closure was based on loving kindness, made possible by Fernanda's clarity of intention.

Sorting out emotions and clarifying intentionality is not only important in romantic relationships. It is crucial when seeking closure in any situation. It lets you make an attempt at mutual understanding and a way forward, rather than unleashing a storm of emotions at the other person. Being clear on your intentionality—

first with yourself and then with others—opens the door to closure.

Intention and the Decision to Walk Away

Intention prepares us to act from a position of strength by helping us be clear with ourselves, which allows us to be clear with others. Sometimes, however, gaining this clarity of intention with ourselves may have an unexpected consequence: it may prompt us to stop seeking closure altogether.

Why? In the process of self-examination, you may decide this is not the best direction for you to go in. Maybe you realize your intention isn't as straightforward as you thought it was. It's not closure you want—you just want the other person to know how you feel, or you just want to get back at them, which will only open the door to more bad behavior on their part (and maybe also yours).

You may recognize that the person you're seeking closure from most likely won't give it to you, and that they may make you feel even worse by denying their role in your pain, attempting to gaslight you, or otherwise causing you more suffering. Why set yourself up for that?

You may come to understand that the closure this person gives you is always temporary and that it's no longer worth your time or energy to keep repeating this cycle. Enough. You've been down that road already and know where it will lead.

You may even decide that you're not yet clear with yourself on why you want closure. Maybe you'll revisit this decision in the future, but for now you haven't sorted out your own feelings well enough to seek closure. The timing is off.

Taking the time to define your intentionality can lead you to any of these decisions. Sometimes the position of strength is to not seek closure. Sometimes the position of strength is to walk away.

Guidelines for Clarifying Your Intentions

Now that you understand the power of intentionality, let's take a closer look at the process of clarifying your intentions with yourself. These step-by-step guidelines will walk you through the process of defining your intentions in a situation where you want closure.

Step One:
Consider the Past

Look at the history of the relationship or situation in question and identify what has brought you to this point in time. Questions to ask yourself in this step include:

- How did we first get connected? What was my first impression of this person? What were my initial instincts about them?
- What have I experienced in this relationship/situation? What aspects did I like or dislike, and why?
- What have I contributed to the relationship, emotionally and in other ways?
- What has the other person contributed?

Step Two:
Examine the Present

Define the emotional pain or dissatisfaction that is causing you to seek closure in the current situation. Questions to ask yourself here include:

- What feels incomplete between us? What loose ends do I want to tie up?
- Can I define this in a way that intuitively feels right to me?
- Can I define this in a way that would be understandable to the other person?

- Is the lack of completeness something I need to work on in myself before I attempt to seek closure?

Step Three:
Define Your Hopes for the Future

Identify how you hope seeking closure will benefit you or the relationship. Some good questions in this step might be:

- What do I want to gain from seeking closure?
- What do I want the other person to understand?
- Will this make our relationship stronger or bring it to an end?
- How does that make me feel? Is that what I really want?

Step Four:
Evaluate Potential Outcomes

Now that you know what kind of closure you want and why, it's time to think about how realistic achieving it might be. Questions at this stage include:

- Given what I know about this person, what are a few ways in which they're most likely to react if I initiate this conversation about closure?
- People can always surprise us. What are some unlikely but still plausible ways this person might react?
- Am I okay with each potential reaction, or would some of them likely make me feel worse and even more incomplete?
- No matter how they react, do I think I'm likely to be able to keep acting with intentionality? In what situations am I most likely to get caught up in my emotions and act in a way I'll later regret?

Step Five:
Decide Your Next Move

Once you've examined your intentions and gotten clarity with yourself and the situation, it's time to choose what action to take. Questions to ask yourself in this step include:

- Do I want to move forward with seeking closure?
- Do I want to give the situation more time?
- Do I want to walk away and not seek closure at all?

You can think of this process as your "pre-closure homework." By doing it, you'll be helping yourself get fully in touch with your feelings and engage your rational mind so you can determine the way forward from a place of strength and empowerment.

EXERCISE:
INTENTIONALITY PRACTICE

Think of a situation or relationship—work, romantic, friendship, family—from the past in which you wanted closure but didn't get it for one reason or another. Sit down in a quiet place with a pen and paper (or computer). Consider this relationship from the position of intentionality. Think through the five steps in the guidelines for clarifying your intentionality, jotting down your responses to the questions in each step.

Once you're done, ask yourself if, in this past situation, you were fully prepared to seek closure from the standpoint of intentionality. Where could your intentions have been clearer, first to yourself and then to the other person? Did you adequately think through your desired outcome, and was it realistic? Did you thoroughly consider how the other person might react, such that you were comfortable with each likely reaction? And finally, ask yourself what you learned about where you most need to be intentional as you seek closure in future relationships.

Be Ready but Don't Rehearse

I always strongly recommend going into a difficult conversation fully prepared, mentally and emotionally. This isn't about manipulating the direction of the conversation with the goal of also manipulating the other person—in fact, the opposite. When you prepare to have a conversation that is based on clear intentions, you are more likely to achieve closure in a way that benefits you and the other person.

First, consider your own readiness. If you've completed your pre-closure homework and really looked inside yourself, you're in a much better position to answer this question. If your emotions are still too raw, if you don't think you can talk about closure without falling apart or blowing up or both, then you may not be ready.

Second, consider the other person's readiness. From what you know about them and where they currently are in life, are they in a place emotionally and mentally where you think they can have this conversation with you? Are they in the midst of life challenges that might render them less receptive to discussing closure with you? Are they still harboring their own feelings about what happened between the two of you, such that they may not even want to talk with you, let alone have what might be a difficult and emotional discussion? Admittedly, you may have no idea if the other person is ready or not. But it's worth considering, and if you think they may not be ready, it may be a good idea to back off for the moment.

Readiness doesn't guarantee success, but considering readiness can place you in a position where success is more likely.

It's important to note, however, that being ready does not mean rehearsing. Often when I speak with a client about their plans for seeking closure, they give a summary of what has led them to this point, why they think closure is important, what they hope to achieve from a closure conversation, and what they believe they can realistically expect from this conversation. So far, so good. But from there, they sometimes begin to describe what the other person will most likely say, and how they'll respond to that, followed by what they'll hear next . . . and so on and so forth. This is what I call rehearsing a conversation.

When you rehearse a conversation you're planning to have, you're setting yourself up for failure. How? You're putting barriers around the conversation by attempting to force it to go by your plan, when in reality we can't force anything to go to plan, least of all other people's behavior. Rather than entering the conversation with an open mind, you're becoming attached to a script. When you have the talk, you'll be listening for key words that will prompt your next response, rather than hearing what the other person is actually saying. The other person, in turn, may not feel they're being listened to, and as a result may shut down or become defensive or argumentative. Outside of the theater, rehearsed conversations are generally a trip to nowhere, even if you think you know the person well enough to predict their responses or if you think you'll be so persuasive they'll have no choice but to respond as you expect them to.

A better approach is to be clear on your intentions but at the same time adopt what is known as beginner's mind. *Beginner's mind* is a term originally from Japanese Zen Buddhism. The idea behind it is that the more you know (or think you know), the less likely you are to be open to learning more—but if you think of yourself as a beginner, even in areas of life where you have a lot of experience, you'll be more open to receiving new, often unexpected knowledge.

Now, apply the concept of beginner's mind to seeking closure. If you rehearse a conversation so much that you go in already "knowing" how it will end, you deny the other person the opportunity to surprise you. But if you speak with honesty and intentionality while keeping an open mind—a beginner's mind—you might well learn something new and unexpected about yourself or the other person.

Closing Thought: Intentionality Is Power

Taking the time to be clear with yourself about your intentions establishes a firm foundation for achieving closure. When we are clear with ourselves regarding our intentions, and clear with the person we're communicating with, we open the door to effective communication. When our intentions are not clear, we open the door to denial, defensiveness, and misunderstanding. Intentionality is the key to achieving closure that is effective, productive, satisfying. Intentionality is power.

Chapter 9

Have the Conversation (or Don't)

Okay, so just how do I have that closure conversation?"
That is a question that I am often asked by my clients. Having a conversation around closure can be uncomfortable, to say the least. Clients talk to me about how they find themselves tongue-tied, stammering, unsure how to say what they want to say. Strong emotions inevitably arise, which makes it even harder to have a conversation. And as I have often discussed, we can't predict how the other person will react.

But that doesn't mean it's impossible. People can and do have conversations about closure, and they can be profoundly meaningful. In chapter 8, we covered how to prepare for such a conversation by examining your emotions and setting your intentions, laying the groundwork for an honest, productive talk. In this chapter, we'll look at best practices for the talk itself—how to say what you need to say and listen to what the other person has to say in order to achieve closure. We'll also look at what to do when a closure conversation is, for whatever reason, not in the cards.

Extending an Invitation

Keep in mind that the worst way to initiate a potentially difficult and emotionally charged conversation is to essentially "ambush" the other person, to take them by surprise by launching directly into this conversation. That's why it's important—and compassionate— to prepare the other person in advance by extending an invitation to talk that lets them know what you want to discuss and why, along with the option to refuse any further discussion.

In general, when you ask to meet with someone to discuss closure, they'll know what you want to talk about before you state your purpose. They may be waiting for you to ask, and want to have this conversation. Or they may be dreading it. And yes, it's also possible that they have no idea what you want to talk with them about.

When you invite the person to have a conversation with you, truly *invite* them. Demanding to have this conversation will lead to defensiveness and make them more likely to refuse, while begging to have the conversation is disempowering to you. So make a simple request, something like: "I would like to sit down with you and have a conversation about our relationship. Will you do that?"

Again, they most likely won't be surprised at your request. People usually know when they have unfinished business with you—but not always! If they ask what you want to talk about, you can respond with something like: "I think you and I would benefit from sitting down and having a conversation together. I have some things I'd like to say to you, and I also want to hear what you have to say to me. Would you be willing to meet? I think we'd both benefit from finding closure with each other."

Ideally you'll get a yes, even if it's tentative. It may include a caveat: "Yes, but I'm not interested in getting into an argument with you," or "Yes, but I hope you're not expecting an apology," or

"Yes, but I'm not going to admit to being at fault," or "Yes, but we're not getting back together."

If you get a maybe, you may have to make another request later, after giving them some time to think about whether they want to speak with you or not.

Or you may get a more direct response: "No." If you get a no, respect it, and accept that you may not find closure, at least not in the way you had hoped. (I'll discuss how to move on without closure more in part 4.)

If the other person accepts your invitation to talk about closure, you'll need to choose a time and place to meet. (I think these conversations are almost always best had in person, but I will discuss alternatives later in this chapter.) You may already have a time and location in mind before you ask the other person to meet, or you may find a mutually comfortable time and location together.

In terms of timing, don't spring this discussion on the other person unexpectedly, and don't ask for a meetup at a time when you know they won't be at their best, such as at the end of a long workday or on a holiday weekend. Schedule a time that is mutually convenient. If the other person feels like they have some input into the meeting time, they'll be more likely to be receptive to having a conversation with you. Nobody likes being inconvenienced, ordered around, or given an ultimatum.

Also consider the place. This can be an emotional discussion, so I would encourage you to choose a venue where you'll be comfortable expressing feelings and where you can speak candidly without being overheard. That means a crowded coffee shop is probably not a good idea, nor is a bustling, noisy restaurant. You may want to meet at your place or theirs, if you can have space to yourself without other people around, but you may not be comfortable being in each other's homes, especially if you have a lot of memories attached. I recommend finding neutral territory, a location that isn't laden with memories and one where you will both feel comfortable, not cornered, not overpowered, not defensive. I'm a big fan of meeting at a public park or taking a walk together, depending on the weather.

Having the Conversation

If, after taking inventory of your emotions and getting clarity on your intentions, you decide to move forward with seeking closure, then comes the big moment: having the conversation. By this time, you may be asking: Why the big buildup? I hope the answer to that question is clear. I always encourage entering into any difficult conversation from a position of strength, empowerment, self-awareness, and compassion. That requires preparation. The following is a step-by-step process to guide you through the closure conversation that I hope will help you with that preparation.

I'll list the steps for the closure conversation here and then go through each one in detail. These steps are not meant as a guarantee that the conversation will go a certain way—remember, over-rehearsing a conversation usually makes it *less* successful, not more—but they should provide a detailed framework to help you think through what you want to say and say it from a place of intentionality and authenticity.

1. State your intentions.
2. Request that the other person listen.
3. State your position using "I" statements.
4. Ask if they understand.
5. Listen to what they have to say.
6. Look for a way forward.

Step One:
State Your Intentions

I have written a lot about the importance of intentionality. If you've gone through the steps in chapter 8, then hopefully you've clarified your intentions to yourself. Stating them out loud to the other person is a good way to get the conversation going.

I recommend starting the conversation out in general terms: "I want to talk about what happened between us. I'd like to talk about what's been going on with me, and I'd like to hear from you."

And then follow with a summary of intention. Examples include:

- "We had a relationship, and now we don't. I don't understand what happened between us, and I'd like to talk with you about it. I feel sad and angry. I'd like to talk to you about what happened from my perspective, and I would like to hear yours."

- "I enjoyed working with you, and I thought of you as someone I could trust. The email you sent caused damage to my reputation. I want to talk about how I feel. I want to know what was going on with you. And I want to see if we can find a way to move forward."

- "We're family. I know that what I said at Thanksgiving dinner didn't sit right with you. I want to clear the air with you. I want you to know why I said it and how I've been feeling since then. I want to know what I can do to mend the tear in our relationship."

Notice in these examples that the speaker, the person seeking closure, is attempting to be clear regarding why they want to have the closure conversation. They are taking ownership of their thoughts and feelings. They are stating their expectations, first to clarify their own perspective and then to hear from the other person. Caution: If your intention is to be heard but not to listen to the other person's side, and you state this directly or indirectly, the conversation may end before it begins.

Step Two:
Request That the Other Person Listen

Once you've stated your intention, request that the other person listen. This is an important next step in your conversation. The operative word here is *request*—not demand, not beg. Simply reiterate that your intention is to have a conversation and ask them to hear what you have to say. This can sound something like: "I'm going to ask you to listen with an open mind. I will do the same for you. Can we have a conversation?" The other person may state their willingness, or they may not. Or they may ask if you can postpone the conversation and have it at a later time. Patience!

Step Three:
State Your Position Using "I" Statements

Now comes the scary part, where you summarize in your own words your perceptions of what happened between the two of you, how you've been impacted, and what you need in order to feel closure. Yes, that means being honest about the feelings you experienced and are continuing to experience. Yes, this is a vulnerable position—you're taking the risk that the other person might not be open to listening or attempting to understand.

First, I want to emphasize the importance of using "I" statements. "I saw . . ." "I think . . ." "I felt . . ." When you use the word *I*, you're taking ownership for how you feel and inviting the other person to listen without defensiveness. On the other hand, starting out with "you" implies that you're going to launch into criticism and accusations, which inevitably causes the other person's walls to go up. The person you're seeking closure from may become defensive regardless of how you attempt to state your position, but "I" statements increase the potential that they'll listen with an open mind.

Additionally, you most likely know this person fairly well, so some emotional intelligence may take you a long way in this conversation in terms of speaking in such a way that the other person can actually hear what you're saying. Choose your words thoughtfully, and be aware of your facial expressions and the tone of your voice. Try not to speak or act in a way you know is likely to trigger a negative response.

When you summarize your perceptions of what happened between the two of you, keep it evidence based. Use specific observations and examples of actions or behaviors that the other person has demonstrated in your relationship, and how you felt as a result. Examples (i.e., evidence) are always easier to understand than generalities, which can more easily be interpreted as accusations. Here are a few brief examples.

- "I thought we were doing really well together and having some great times. I thought we were learning a lot about each other, especially how to be a couple. After you moved in, I felt like we started gradually becoming more distant from each other. I didn't get the feeling you wanted to hear what I had to say anymore or to spend time with me. You worked late into the evening. You made plans with your family that no longer included me. I felt unloved. I was devastated."

- "The project we were working on together seemed to be progressing well. We were meeting our monthly goals and getting some good feedback from management. I tried to be open with you about where I thought we needed additional resources, and I thought you agreed with me. So when you sent the memo around calling me out for missing a project milestone, I was frankly shocked. I got a nasty reprimand from the director. I am deeply disappointed. I feel like I was made the scapegoat."

- "I had a little too much to drink before Thanksgiving dinner. I own that. And I haven't made it a secret how I feel about your marriage breaking up, about how I had hoped the two of you would try harder to make it work. Of course, I know this was your relationship and not mine, and you have your own reasons for making the decision you made. But when I made the comment about the empty place at the table and who you might try to fill it with next year, I was sober enough to know I was totally out of line. I could see it in your face."

As you read these examples, you may notice that the speaker is speaking from the "I," not the accusatory and critical "you." While we can't assume anything where other people are concerned, the listener is hopefully able to at least hear and take in the conversation so far. Being able to state your position this clearly takes preparation. If the speaker in these scenarios had not taken the time to sort out their thoughts and feelings, and to pair them with specific examples, these summaries might have been essentially emotional outbursts—yelling, crying, accusations, and defensiveness, leading nowhere.

By the way, if the other person attempts to interrupt you to argue a point or otherwise defend themselves, I advise you to ask them to please listen until you've finished what you have to say. And then remind them that you're also here to listen to them. If it's clear that they're truly unable to listen, save yourself further heartache and frustration and end the conversation.

Step Four:
Ask If They Understand

After you've stated your position and clarified your thoughts and feelings, ask the other person if they understand what you're trying to convey. This can be as simple as "Do you understand what I'm saying?" or "Does this make sense to you?" Be prepared for some defensiveness—or a lot of defensiveness. No one likes to hear that they're less than perfect. If you encounter resistance, you may want to add something like, "I'm not asking you to agree with me. I'm just asking you to understand."

In a perfect world, you would have some assurance that the person you're seeking closure with at least understands, even if they disagree or feel compelled to defend themselves. You may also find that they're not able to continue the conversation. They may agree to pick it up again later, or they may not.

Step Five:
Listen to What They Have to Say

The offer to be a listener as well as a speaker is essential in any conversation. You were listened to; now it is your turn to listen. So make an offer: "I would like to hear your thoughts and how you're feeling about what I said." Notice I didn't say "I would like to hear your side." Calling out "sides" might imply that this is a battle and only one of you can be right. Inviting the other person to express themselves implies that you want to work together.

If they are willing to express their perspective, then honor them by listening. You may have to work with yourself, maybe do some calming breathing, to help you listen with an open mind and not jump in to argue or otherwise become defensive. Hopefully they approach the conversation from a place of authenticity and intentionality as well. However, if they behave irrationally or abusively, or if you find yourself experiencing more of the behavior that has led you to seek closure in the first place, then you may have to decide to end the conversation (and potentially accept that the closure you were hoping for isn't possible).

Step Six:
Look for a Way Forward

The closure you need may simply be to talk about your perceptions of what happened between the two of you and how you felt. Of course, this is seldom simple. You talk about what you need the other person to know, maybe they describe their reactions and add their own thoughts and feelings, and you resolve those lingering questions and tie up loose ends—closure. However, a question is most likely still hanging in the air: "So, what's next?" Or more directly: "What do you want from me?"

Closure may close a door and end a relationship. It may open a door to a way forward. The conversation that follows may be no conversation beyond a decision to part ways. Or, with the air now clear, it may be about working together on a way forward, making agreements and promises.

Whatever it is, it needs to be clearly stated, as in these examples:

- "After what has happened between us, I don't think we have a relationship anymore, at least not one that works for me. So I can't continue in our relationship. I want you to know why and to hopefully understand."

- "I hear what you're saying about why you did what you did. But we have to continue to work together. Can we talk about how to do that going forward?"

- "We are family. That will never change. But I know I hurt you and made you angry. Can you find it in your heart to forgive me?"

Your intention for seeking closure may be to maintain your relationship, continuing on in a more emotionally healthy or productive manner, based on an agreement of how one or both of you will make changes. If so, some back-and-forth will be required. Talking, listening, understanding each other. If you have been honest and specific about why you're seeking closure, as well as clear about what you want, you will be more likely to find common ground. Closure may be the door opener to working harder and more intentionally on your relationship.

I know this isn't easy if you're in a lot of emotional pain. It's probably not easy for the other person either. It's possible they may need to take some time to digest and consider what you have said. They may be surprised, angry, hurt, or experiencing other feelings they need time to process. If so, offer to pick up the conversation at a later time when they're more ready to speak. However, at the same time, don't get caught in the trap of repeatedly seeking closure as a way to maintain a relationship that is essentially on life support when the plug needs to be pulled.

Having said that, the act of describing your perceptions of what occurred and how you felt may be all the closure you need, regardless of how the other person reacts. Sometimes we just need to get it out of our system, and in the process of letting it out, we also realize that's all we needed to do. If so, you said what you needed to say. End the conversation and get on with your life.

Don't Use Closure as a Weapon

I can't leave the topic of the closure conversation without asking you to consider how you may intentionally or unintentionally be using closure as a weapon against someone else.

Insisting on a conversation about closure can feel empowering at first. You charge in with guns blasting and demand to be apologized to, validated, understood. The problem is that the other person may not see it that way. So forcing the conversation can lead you to a wall of defensiveness, denial, downright stubbornness. You may find yourself going back to have the same conversation and make the same demands, and continuing to come up empty-handed. All that empowerment wears down over time as you begin to feel you're hollering into an echo chamber and hearing the same tired argument echoing back to you. Also keep in mind the other person may feel bullied or even abused. Your need to be right may be causing them deep emotional harm and disempowerment.

If you find yourself trying to use a closure conversation as a way to prove you're right or make the other person feel bad, you may need to go back to the drawing board, starting with examining whether your intentions are based on faulty, irrational thinking. It might be a better use of your time to walk away. But keep in mind that if you've caused someone emotional pain, you may also need to ask forgiveness to help both of you heal.

Conversely, what about when someone is asking *you* for closure? Wow, the rush of power! Finally, you're in the driver's seat. How will you use that power? Will you decide to leave the other person to sit with their feelings? Consider your motivation. Maybe this is a door you don't want to open again. Maybe you know this person and suspect this may be yet another attempt at manipulation or intimidation. Maybe you want to dole out some punishment to someone you feel has harmed you who you don't think deserves closure. Or will you hear them out, consider their perspective, and give them what closure you can, and maybe give yourself some closure as well? You may decide the issue for which the other person is seeking closure is one that you don't want to revisit, that might be harmful to you emotionally. It's all in your hands.

The way to avoid using closure as a weapon in any scenario is to act out of compassion. Listen to your instincts. Protect your own emotions from being damaged. Choose the route that will most benefit the future of your relationship with the other person or provide an ending that can result in mutual healing.

Nonverbal Communication, Unspoken Closure

In my experience, in my own life and with my clients, there are many potential reasons for not sitting down with someone and talking to them about closure. Some of these reasons you might identify with. Maybe the other person is usually argumentative, defensive, or even abusive, and you don't want to submit yourself to that anymore. On the other hand, you may also fear that having a discussion around closure could be harmful to them. You may be feeling so much emotional pain that you can't even imagine trying to verbalize how you feel, and fear you will fall apart in front of someone you don't want to fall apart in front of. Or they may flat out refuse to speak with you.

But not all communication is verbal, and not all closure comes through conversation. In the second half of this chapter, we'll cover unspoken closure—seeking closure when sitting down and having a conversation is, for whatever reason, impossible.

When people talk about nonverbal forms of seeking closure, I often hear words of judgment. "What a coward!" "How passive-aggressive!" "That was so cold!" At times, these judgments are not unreasonable. Like any attempt at closure, the nonverbal kind can leave more pain and frustration in its wake.

But I also have to say this: We are all human. We all have limitations. We are all doing the best we can, even if what we do is far from anybody's concept of "best." We're all out there in the world trying to figure things out. Consequently, sometimes nonverbal communication is all we can do. Sure, unspoken closure can be ineffective, leaving behind the pain and frustration of loose ends. However, expressing your intentions in a profound way, transcending the limits of the words that you didn't have available to you, can also be healing.

Unspoken closure can come in many forms. As we take a look at some of them, I suspect you will be reminded of examples of closure in your own life that didn't involve spoken words.

A Smile, a Frown

A look can say it all. Sometimes that's all you need to feel closure. Other times, that's about all you're going to get.

You've probably had the experience of going through a rough time with someone. The pain may have been so great that you or the other person just couldn't talk about it. You didn't want to re-hash it all, to bring up the memories and emotions. Or maybe you heard them out but had nothing to say in return. You may also have had the experience of just getting worn out on talking about something.

What about a smile? Smiling connects us with another person. It says: "We're okay." "I understand you." "I forgive you." A smile, if it's sincere, can heal wounds. But keep in mind that a smile can also be sad. It can signify that we tried but we have to part ways. Our closure is to agree to disagree and move on. The relationship was good when it was good, and there are memories of this person you'll always cherish. A sad smile says it in ways that words can't.

Other facial expressions can have a very different impact. A frown or an angry look can end communication. It can be the cherry on the cake of an attempt at closure that was unsuccessful or, on the other hand, the clincher in closure that was successful but left one or both of you with bad feelings. A frown can say, "Yes, we are done with each other, and I am well rid of you." It can drive the message home and close the door to further attempts. A blank expression can have the same results.

A Hug, a Pat

In mental health, we often talk about the importance of touch. So much can be conveyed by a hug, a pat on the shoulder, a handshake.

Think about the last time you hugged someone. What meaning did it convey to you? "I care about you." "I appreciate you." "I understand." "I don't agree with you, but we're still okay." "I forgive you." "I hope you forgive me." Hugging someone can be a way to reassure them after you've had a conversation, to let them know that everything is fine between you. Hugging can also be a way to say goodbye, temporarily or forever.

A pat can work the same way. Giving someone a pat on the hand or the shoulder can be reassuring in the same way as a hug. You might pat someone in passing, a small gesture that can mean a lot to both of you. You might pat someone when a hug would not be comfortable or appropriate, depending on the relationship you have with that person.

Have you ever been in a closure-related situation in which there just wasn't anything else to say? Maybe you had reached an impasse, neither of you were getting the closure you had hoped for, you didn't understand each other, or you didn't agree. But you also didn't want this to be the end of the relationship. If so, you might have found that hugging it out or giving the other person a pat on the shoulder gave you both closure when your words weren't up to the task.

Of course, the other side of conveying a message with physical touch is smacking someone or otherwise causing physical harm. There are way too many examples of attempting to seek closure through a slap across the face or a punch in the nose. If you haven't experienced it in life—and hopefully you haven't—you have most likely seen it in the movies. In a culture of anger, people all too often try to find closure through causing someone else physical pain and the humiliation that may accompany it. It might feel good in the moment, but it's not a healthy way to find closure, and the results are seldom satisfactory for either person in the long run.

Putting It in Writing

While many of us have abandoned the art of letter writing, we seem to have replaced it with email and text messages. I have had many clients over the years who end a relationship over text, including discussing the whys and hows that I normally associate with an in-person closure conversation. Either they were avoiding meeting in person or they didn't feel they needed to. In their case, texting was enough. I have seen email used the same way. Sometimes closure occurs through a lot of back-and-forth emailing, other times with one clear (or not-so-clear) email message.

I personally think that electronic communication is a poor substitute for getting together and talking things out in real time. There is a time delay between each response, especially with emailing, though people may also wait a day or two to respond to a text. Some people are better writers than others, better at expressing their thoughts and feelings. Tone of voice and facial expressions are absent, which can lead to incorrect assumptions and can unintentionally steer the conversation in a direction that is potentially destructive.

However, I also understand that in-person conversation is not always possible. So if you're going to attempt getting closure through an email, I recommend a brief, clearly stated summary of your intentions, what you experienced, and how you feel. The written word can be powerful. The other person may understand by reading, and rereading, in ways they couldn't have in a conversation. People don't always listen if they're defensive and intent on planning their comeback. When they read, they have time to digest and sort out their reactions. So in this way, texting or emailing can be beneficial.

However, be prepared for anything. For the reasons I mentioned, you may receive a response that is totally unexpected, leaving you to try to reframe the discussion or repair the damage. Chances are that the closure you were hoping for is less likely to be achieved. Also, it is my experience with texting and email that each person wants to have the last word, even if they're words of kindness. Consequently, your attempt at closure may instead open up an ongoing volley of words, potentially angry ones. This can have the effect of introducing more toxicity into your life when you were hoping for just the opposite.

Additionally, blocking someone's number or account is possible in the virtual world in a way it isn't in the offline world. If the other person chooses to block you, then you might well be left feeling *more* misunderstood, abused, disrespected, or whatever else you were feeling, with no opportunity to resume communication. You may feel worse than you felt before.

And one more thing. Text messages and emails are permanent records. They can be passed from one person to another, so your business may end up out in the open in ways that you don't want it to be, and your words may come back to haunt you.

The old-fashioned letter can also be effective. Sorting out your thoughts in a letter, just as in electronic communication, can help you clarify how you feel, first for yourself and then for the other person. You may receive a response, and you may not. I personally think a letter is best used to end communication, to achieve closure that is all about you finally stating how you feel and what you want and don't want. Most likely, you and the other person will not be volleying letters back and forth to each other, though if that is your intention, then a letter may serve this purpose well. As with electronic communication, letters (and photos of letters) can be passed around among friends, so make sure you're okay with that possibility.

Returning Possessions

We attach memories to our possessions. I certainly do. If you look around your home, you might see many items that were given to you by someone who is, or was, important to you. If you had a falling-out with this person, would you want to be reminded of them by seeing the gift they gave you? You might keep it if it has value to you, even if the relationship no longer does. Or it might be a sad reminder of someone you lost, through a falling-out or by death. If you were angry enough at this person, or hurt, or disappointed, and wanted to make a statement of your own, you might also consider sending the item back to them.

Let me tell you a story here. A friend of mine, Keisha, had finally admitted to herself that her longtime friend Nadine was a narcissist. Nadine constantly called Keisha to talk about her own problems, her own relationships, her own children, without offering any support in return. Sometimes these conversations would go on for hours. Keisha finally decided she'd had enough. She called and told Nadine that she could no longer be in contact with her. Nadine just hung up on her. No apology, no request for an explanation, no attempt at setting the friendship right. Only silence.

A few days later, Keisha received a large box in the mail. She saw the package was from Nadine, so out of curiosity and for old times' sake, she looked forward to seeing what was inside. When she opened the package, she saw that her former friend had returned most of the birthday gifts Keisha had given her over the years. No note, no explanation. But then, no explanation was needed. Keisha had sought closure by stating why she could no longer be in contact, and Nadine had sought closure by sending a box of old birthday gifts, cash on delivery. Nadine probably felt the short-lived rush of revenge, not true closure, but while Keisha was disappointed, this action did tie up loose ends for her. She understood that her friend's fragile ego had been wounded and that she had made the right choice by disconnecting from her.

Do I recommend this approach to closure over sitting down and having a conversation? Not really. But I also understand that sometimes a door needs to be closed and we do the best we can to close it.

Silence

In my line of work, I have many conversations with clients who talk about trying to find closure through the silent treatment. "I'll show my partner they can't treat me that way anymore. I won't speak to them for a few days." "After she did that to me, I decided never to talk to her again. I cut off all communication." "I guess he doesn't want to see me anymore. I got ghosted."

Conversations around closure are often not easy, as I have said before. It's human nature, when words are lacking, to go silent. What are the reasons behind the silent act? You may be so mad or sad that you just can't put it into words. You may fear the other person can't or won't understand. Your emotions may be over-flowing, and you want to avoid the potential of falling apart. However, as you may have experienced in your own life, going silent is all too often a way of punishing the person.

Silence is not always golden. Cutting off communication leaves a sense of incompleteness behind. In the absence of information, our mind creates a story for us, often the worst-case scenario. In your silence, the echo chamber of your mind may re-create the situation that resulted in going silent. Memories may become cloudy and consequently reimagined. The facts may change. Your reasons for going silent may shift and change. You may find yourself re-playing past events or rehearsing a conversation with the person you want closure from.

This isn't to say that it can't be helpful to take a break and give each other some space before you come back together and talk things out. However, the longer the silence continues, the less likely you are to find the closure you need with this person. The result is a missed opportunity—for personal growth and healing, for closing one chapter so that you can begin a new one, or for repairing a relationship so that you can move forward.

Having said that, as the saying goes, the best way to deal with a schoolyard bully is to walk away. Sometimes silence is your best, or only, option. If you can't get closure in a way that benefits you and doesn't lead to further wounds, it's time to walk away.

Acts of Kindness

One scenario in which you definitely can't find closure through a conversation is when a loved one dies. But that doesn't mean closure is impossible. I often talk with clients about finding closure by honoring the legacy of a lost loved one through acts of kindness. You may have had this conversation yourself. You can honor someone's memory in many ways. You can give to a charity your loved one valued or that would benefit a community of which they were a member. You can create an event or a scholarship in their honor. Or you can simply choose to be kinder as a way of emulating the kindness you experienced from your loved one. This is another way of helping you to find some closure as you cope with grief, a way to help make sense of your loss.

Acts of kindness can also provide closure in other situations. You may feel guilt and shame over something you did. Maybe you weren't able to receive forgiveness from the person you harmed and you feel you still need to take some kind of positive action to achieve closure. Or maybe you didn't harm anyone directly, but you still feel bad about an action you took. You might have some fond memories of someone who touched you in some way, at work or in your community, who you weren't able to properly thank. Performing an act of kindness, paying it forward, can help provide closure on a deep and meaningful level. It might even open new doors to connections and self-expression, a new chapter that you weren't expecting.

EXERCISE:
PRACTICING THE CLOSURE CONVERSATION

Think about a current situation in your life that presents an opportunity to find closure with another person. Review all the steps in the "Having the Conversation" section and jot down what you might say to this person at each step. (Remember, the purpose of this exercise is to plan what you intend to say, not to rehearse what you expect or want to happen.) Now take some time and sort through the feelings that came up for you as you worked through the steps in the conversation. Ask yourself:

- Am I clear on my intentions, such that I can state them and feel comfortable that I'm speaking from the heart?
- How confident do I feel that the other person will be able to respond as I hope they do?
- Did I identify any steps that might be especially uncomfortable for the other person or for me? Is there something I can do or say to help us both feel more comfortable and open?
- How confident do I feel that I can be open to what the other person has to say, that I can listen without attempting to force them to respond as I want them to?
- Now that I've taken the time to be more specific about what I want to say, am I ready for this conversation? Do I still feel it will be beneficial, or is it time to walk away from closure?

Closing Thought:
You Got This!

It's hard to ask for something you want and need. It means opening yourself up, being vulnerable with another person, exposing yourself, asking to be heard and hopefully understood. That can be a lot.

It might help you overcome any hesitation to consider the benefit of letting the other person know how you feel and why, of taking ownership of your thoughts and feelings. By expressing yourself, you're no longer holding all of this inside. It's all out there. Finally. That can be empowering.

Sure, you may not receive the closure you want. You may not be understood. You may feel like you're talking at a wall. You may experience more of what caused you to seek closure directed back at you.

But have courage! What does courage mean? Being compassionate while also being honest and direct. Saying what you need to say. Listening to truths you might not want to hear. Being willing to look for the common ground, if one can be found, and accepting when the common ground can't be found because the other person isn't willing to join you in looking. Courage also means accepting when it's time to walk away, which we'll discuss further in part 4.

Chapter 10

Evaluate

After attempting to achieve closure, you are left with a question: How did it go? Now that we've covered preparing for a conversation about closure in chapter 8 and having the conversation in chapter 9, it's time to evaluate the results of the conversation.

Did you receive the closure you thought you wanted and needed? Did you receive closure in a way you didn't expect? Or did your effort to find closure fail?

Before you answer, take a step back and review the conversation as you might review a videotape: what you said, what they said, and where you ended up. If the conversation was so painful you don't even want to think about it again, use some mindfulness techniques. Do some calming breathing and then visualize the conversation based on your memory of how it went. You might even consider writing about it; this can help with recall.

As you consider whether or not you received closure, keep the focus on you. I know it's not always easy to do if you feel haunted by the emotions the other person expressed, but I recommend you focus on your own reactions, not theirs.

What does your rational mind tell you about the experience?

Objectively, do you think you have closure? On the other hand, take your emotional temperature. Do you feel in your gut that you got what you needed from this conversation? If your emotions are all over the place, you may need to sit with them for a while before you can more accurately assess the outcome. This chapter will help you sort through your thoughts and feelings, gain some perspective, and determine whether you've been able to achieve closure—and what comes next.

How Are You Feeling?

Humans are emotional beings. Most likely, a big motivator for seeking closure was to help you cope with strong feelings or, to say it another way, to help yourself feel better. Feelings were most likely interwoven into your intentionality—not necessarily your sole intention, but certainly factored in, consciously or unconsciously. Below are some of the feelings my clients often talk to me about and that I have experienced myself. Reading through them may help you to identify some of your own feelings.

- **Happiness:** You most likely feel happiness if you successfully achieved the closure you wanted. You said what you needed to say. The other person listened, seemed to sincerely understand you, and reacted in a way that you needed them to react. Now, this is certainly the ideal closure, but it's not exactly the most common outcome, at least according to the experiences of my clients and myself. Still, you might also feel happy for other reasons, such as feeling happy that you finally allowed yourself to express your anger.

- **Sadness:** Talking with someone about finding closure can be a sad experience. Speaking about past problems may mean reexperiencing old feelings of sadness, for example. Also, the conversation will bring up emotions in the other person. If they react badly and you don't achieve closure, you might feel sad about that. If they react with sadness, you may also feel sad, even if you do achieve closure. You may feel sad when closure entails ending a relationship, changing the way you'll interact with someone in the future, or acknowledging the end of a life. Endings are not always happy endings, even when we're able to tie up those loose ends.

- **Anger:** As with sadness, anger can come from within or can be a response to how the other person feels. The process of seeking closure may be the moment when you finally allow yourself to feel the anger that you've been suppressing. The anger may rise to the surface when you tell the other person what you've experienced in your relationship that has finally brought you to this point. If expressed appropriately, anger can be liberating. However, you may also experience anger resulting from how the other person behaves during the conversation—for example, if they refuse to acknowledge your feelings, attempt to gaslight you, react to you with their own anger, and so on.

- **Fear:** You may walk away from a closure conversation fearful that you harmed the other person emotionally, or afraid of how they may react (or worse, retaliate) down the line. You may walk away afraid of your own behavior and what it says about you—the way your anger came out, the things you said, the thoughts you had. ("Wow, I didn't know I had that in me.") Fear is hard to sit with, and it may motivate you to go back and try to seek closure a second time. But as you may have experienced in other areas of your life, acting out of fear usually doesn't lead to results that are productive or beneficial to yourself or the other person.

- **Guilt/shame:** Feelings of guilt and shame are often wrapped around other emotions in the wake of a closure conversation. Anger can lead to a sense of shame. ("Why did I say that?") You may feel some guilt if you're happy and the other person isn't. You may be ashamed of how scared you feel. ("Aren't I braver than that?") However, guilt and shame can stand by themselves as well. They can stem from self-criticism or a sense that you don't deserve to feel closure, especially if you pushed yourself out of your comfort zone to have the conversation or are accustomed to feeling like a victim. Shame may be immediate, but it may also arise over time as your own feelings emerge and as you become aware of how the other person is reacting.

- **Frustration:** If the conversation didn't go the way you wanted it to, you might feel plain old frustration. Other people don't always behave the way we'd like them to. Maybe this person refused to talk about what you needed to talk about. Or they refused to hear you out. Or they didn't understand. Or they made you out to be a bad guy as a way to absolve themselves of responsibility. And on and on. The danger here is that this frustration can lead you to continue to come back for more attempts at closure, further disempowering yourself and making yourself more unhappy.

- **Relief:** Relief is a common emotion when a closure conversation goes well, but my clients also often talk about how just making the attempt gave them a sense of relief, even if it wasn't everything they'd hoped for. You might feel relief because you asserted yourself, were open about your feelings, let someone know what it was like to be treated the way they treated you. At least you got it out in the open. And as previously stated, getting closure can mean that you resolved your ambiguities, even if you're not exactly thrilled with the outcome. Getting that kind of closure, even if it's not ideal, may give you a sense of relief because now you can stop fixating on the situation and move on with your life.

If you have difficulty identifying your feelings, give yourself time. Whenever you have an emotional encounter with another person, it can be helpful to take some time to recover. A closure conversation is no different. Above all, be patient with yourself and show yourself some compassion. And don't go through this alone. Gather your support team around you. Talk it out. Yell it out. Cry it out. Sit down with the people in your life who you trust, who know you, who have your back. In the process of explaining a situation so that someone who is not part of it can understand what's happening and how you're being impacted, you also better reframe it for yourself. (In fact, that's one of the benefits of talk therapy!)

What Are You Thinking?

Our emotions are closely related to our thoughts, so as we examine what we're feeling, we also have to examine what we're thinking. Note that I'm using *thoughts* here as an umbrella term to include not only specific thoughts but also your perceptions, your beliefs, your worldview. We all have beliefs that we've internalized during our life due to our family of origin, our communities, our cultures. Some cause us pain; some are great strengths.

Suppose you initiate a conversation about closure that doesn't go as well as you hoped, and you're left with feelings that anyone would have in your position: anger, sadness, frustration. Consider what thoughts might arise alongside and in relation to these feelings, consciously or unconsciously. Here are some examples of self-defeating or irrational thoughts that I often encounter with my clients.

- "This always happens to me. Yet again, I am misunderstood and disrespected."
- "The other person knew I was going to bring this up and they rehearsed their attack so they could get one over on me."
- "I'm going to be forced to swallow my feelings and feel awful about this forever."
- "Yet another toxic person is making me miserable—story of my life."
- "People really are basically unkind, as if I needed more evidence."
- "Back to the drawing board. Next time, I'll be the first to go on the attack!"

Thoughts like these are essentially dark clouds that sit on your shoulder, waiting for a chance to rain on you. You don't *try* to have them. They're the result of your upbringing, your basic personality makeup, and the experiences you've had over the years, among other factors. You don't necessarily consider these thoughts or form them rationally; they jump up and give you a big assist interpreting the situation you find yourself in. Unfortunately, they often "assist" you in feeling even worse. Mental health professionals refer to these as irrational beliefs, thoughts that are not necessarily based on reality but have been programmed into our brains over the years.

Attempting to find closure with someone based on an irrational belief about yourself is setting yourself up for frustration, disappointment, disempowerment. When my clients are struggling with irrational beliefs that keep popping up to distort their perceptions, cause them emotional pain, and otherwise interfere with their peace of mind, I encourage them to drag those beliefs into an imaginary courtroom.

How does this work? Think of a potentially irrational belief that you're holding as you seek closure. Then imagine yourself in a court of law, being harangued by a nasty prosecutor who rips into you with one of your self-defeating beliefs—for example, "You never get what you want," or "You will never be loved." Finally, your defense attorney says, "Objection! Just what is the evidence here? My client has never once in their life been loved? My client has never once received what they wanted? Really? These accusations don't hold water. These are irrational beliefs!"

Take a moment and consider your self-defeating belief from this perspective. Is it absolutely always true? And a more important question: Is it possible that it doesn't have to always be true?

The judge intervenes at this point: "With no evidence, the case is dismissed. You can all go home."

Have some fun with this, but take the time to fully answer your defense attorney's questions. Just what *is* the evidence? Is it possible that the word *sometimes* would be more accurate than the words *always* or *never*? And is it possible that, with some work on your part, you can end this cycle going forward?

If your need for closure is based on an irrational belief like the ones above, the next step is to ask yourself: What am I hoping to achieve through closure? Am I trying to get closure as a way to prove or disprove an irrational belief? If so, you're essentially asking another person to let you off the hook for your own internally generated self-criticism, which probably means you're setting yourself up for disempowerment, no growth, and further emotional pain.

In my experience with my clients, our thoughts are all too often critical, judgmental, focused on what's bad rather than what's good. But our beliefs and perceptions don't have to be negative. We also have thoughts that give us encouragement, are self-affirming, help us see the bright side, guide us toward deciding the cup is half-full and moving on. Yes, these beliefs, also referred to as rational beliefs, can help us to achieve closure and to feel a sense of satisfaction, or at least acceptance and the confidence to walk away from closure.

The Power of Rational Mind

So what are we supposed to do to help ourselves achieve closure if we can't rely on our own thoughts and feelings? Let's start here: You are not your feelings; they're just feelings. You are not your thoughts; they're just thoughts. What's reliable is your rational mind!

Rational mind is a concept used in several different schools of thought, from Buddhism to Western psychology; I became familiar with it while studying rational emotive behavior therapy (REBT) at the Albert Ellis Institute. You can visualize rational mind as sitting on top of your thoughts and feelings, which helps you to sort through both of them. Rational mind lets you identify the feelings you're experiencing and to name them: anger, sadness, fear. It helps you identify that the thoughts are causing the emotions you're feeling: this thought leads to that emotion. Rational mind helps you evaluate whether those thoughts are realistic and productive, if they promote your sense of self-worth, if they help you to be kind to yourself . . . or if they're all about creating worst-case scenarios, criticizing yourself, making yourself feel like a victim.

Now, rational mind may also ultimately help you to see where the other person had a point, or where your reactions, even your need for closure, were based on faulty perceptions of the situation or irrational beliefs. Rational mind may help you decide that while you didn't receive the closure you had hoped for, you did receive closure, even if only because you were able to say how you felt regardless of how the other person reacted. And your rational mind may guide you in determining that no, you did not receive closure, and it's time to move on with your life in a different way.

Rational mind doesn't always give us the conclusion we would most prefer. But it can save us from being mired in anger and resentment and hate.

EXERCISE:
ENGAGING RATIONAL MIND

How do you engage rational mind? First, go off by yourself someplace where you can think and feel without distraction. Take a few calming breaths; this is a great way to awaken rational mind, by helping you quiet your emotions and confusing thoughts and to get into a mental space where you can more effectively sort through them. Then, imagine yourself as standing outside of yourself, observing this person who is trying to pull themselves out of the mud of messy thoughts and feelings. Ask yourself some questions:

- How am I feeling? Name your feelings.
- What thoughts am I having about what happened?
- How are these thoughts connected to each of these feelings?
- Do I hold beliefs about my place in the world that are rational and support my emotional wellness? Do I hold beliefs about my place in the world that are not rational and, consequently, steal my peace of mind?

> • And finally: If these are not rational, realistic
> evaluations of the situation, am I repeating
> thoughts and feelings that often come up for me in
> difficult situations?

If You Didn't Achieve Closure

As I have stated previously, humans don't like loose ends. If we attempt closure and aren't successful, we're left with a whole new set of loose ends. "He really said this?" "She really did that?" "They think what?" This can be hard to sit with. So hard, in fact, that you may be tempted to give it another try.

It's human nature to want the last word. We've all had moments when we felt that way, fantasized about it, rehearsed it. Maybe as you think back on your closure conversation, you identify where you let your guard down, what you should have said but didn't have the presence of mind to say. But beware of that little voice in the back of your mind whispering, "Now I know what I *really* need to say are angry words that would have put the other person in their place or kinder words that would have better described your feelings."

If this is you, no need for self-criticism. It's a normal reaction. But following that impulse usually doesn't lead to closure. If you find yourself strategizing on how to have the last word, you may be heading into a trap. When you need to have the last word, you risk:

• Trying to be right when the other person is only going to insist they're right. This is a lose-lose situation that is most likely going to keep all those uncomfortable feelings stirred up.

- Trying to be right when maybe you aren't ready to see the other person's side. You may have a lesson to learn about yourself, but so much has occurred between the two of you that you're beyond the point of being able to come to a mutual understanding that might lead to growth for both of you.

- Getting caught up in trying to control how the other person responds to your attempt at closure, leaving you wanting to do it right the next time around, as if you had the power to control another person's reactions in the first place.

- Opening the door to creating a tit-for-tat competition that can devolve into a grudge match and revenge. Do you really need to bring this toxicity into your life?

None of this will bring you any closer to long-lasting, healthy closure. Instead it will trap you in a cycle of trying for closure "one more time" (unless you fail again, and then one *more* time).

A similar thought process often plays out in the form of nagging doubts about how the conversation went. Whether the conversation went well overall or not, it probably didn't play out like a movie script—because it wasn't a movie, it was real life. Especially if you didn't achieve the closure you wanted, you may be plagued by nagging doubts about what you should have said or done differently that might have resulted in a different outcome.

Did you say what you needed to say, based on your intentions for seeking closure? Did the other person understand? Did they respond the way you hoped they would? Did they respond in one of the alternate ways that you also thought might be possible?

If you were able to answer yes to the first question—meaning you were able to say what you needed to say—then you did the best you could do. How the other person reacted is out of your control. So put the nagging doubts to rest and move forward on a different path.

What's Next for Your Relationship?

Whether you feel you actually achieved closure or not, a conversation about closure will have an effect on your relationship with the person in question. The effect might be to end the relationship, as difficult as that might be. If you're continuing the relationship, that comes with its own set of challenges. You may need to take some time to cautiously implement the changes you have mutually decided to make, giving each other the necessary space to do so.

Navigating the closure journey with a romantic partner or a friend is of course complicated. You both have choices to make in terms of what you need to do to protect your own emotional health, as well as the health of your relationship. But you do have choices.

The choices available in other kinds of relationships may be more limited. At work, unless you quit your job, you may still need to be in contact with the individual with whom you sought closure or didn't find closure. Hopefully you figured out a way to interact moving forward. Similarly, family members are still your family; nothing changes that. Even if you decide to cut off contact—and sometimes this is necessary in a toxic family—then the nature of your relationship will change, but because you share relatives, you may not be able to completely avoid interacting with them. If you don't cut off contact, again, you will need to find a way forward together.

Changing the dynamic of personal relationships doesn't happen overnight. It happens day by day, through trial and error and being true to your original intentions (yes, that intention word again). Remember: patience and compassion, for yourself and the other person.

Is the Other Person Okay?

Sometimes what we get when we seek closure is too much of what we thought would be a good thing. Maybe you wanted the other person to admit they were wrong and apologize to you, but you didn't necessarily want to see them crumble into a puddle, scramble for words, or beg for forgiveness. If this happens, you may have the experience of coming away from a conversation around closure with some lingering feelings of guilt and shame. The example that comes to mind first is a romantic breakup, but this can happen in any number of situations—ending a friendship because the other person is too self-absorbed and then discovering they cared more about the relationship than you realized, letting a coworker know you won't continue to cover for them and then finding out they're on probation and desperate to keep their job.

Beware of where guilt and shame can take you. Trying to resolve these feelings can lead you right back to the original relationship problems, with an attempt to "make it up" to the other person resulting in the same unhealthy interactions that caused the need for closure in the first place. It's like setting yourself up for more punishment to resolve your guilt and shame, as a way to replace the original feelings the relationship brought up for you.

So use rational mind here. Take a look at your guilt and shame, and at the thoughts and perceptions that are coming up for you. Think about how you might help a friend in a similar situation, what you would ask them, the advice you might give. And think about what a compassionate response might look like—one that's compassionate toward yourself as well as the other person.

You may decide that a check-in in the form of a brief call or a note, with a few words like "I hope you're okay" or "I wish you the best," is the kindest thing to do. You might encourage the other person to get the support that you aren't able to provide without placing your own emotional wellness at risk. But keep in mind that reengaging is often *not* the best thing to do after you've achieved closure with someone, unless the closure you achieved has opened the door to improving and even deepening your relationship. If closure means closing a door, it is advisable *not* to reengage to the extent that you'll risk stirring things up again. Sometimes the compassionate thing to do in this case is to allow the other person the freedom to feel their own feelings, to let them rely on their own resilience and resources without stepping in and trying to fix them, which can be ultimately disempowering for both of you.

Look for the Lesson

When you go through an emotional experience, it leaves a gift behind, though it may not seem like one at the time. The gift comes in the form of a lesson. If you're open to learning it, you learn something about how you think, feel, behave. You learn about emotional buttons that can easily be pushed by people and situations. You learn more about what you want and don't want in life, as well as what you want and don't want in the people you decide to allow into your life. You learn what to do and what not to do to get what you need. And for better or for worse, you learn more about what you can and can't expect from other people.

The act of seeking closure can be a lesson in and of itself. You learn why you were in the position of wanting closure with another person. What led you there. What you contributed to the situation and what the other person contributed.

These can be hard lessons, but they're valuable. Life has provided you with yet another opportunity to grow.

EXERCISE:
TAKE A LOOK AT YOUR RATIONAL BELIEFS

I have talked about irrational beliefs in this chapter. But I also referenced rational beliefs as well. So how about carving out some time to take a closer look at your rational beliefs? Just as a quick review, rational beliefs are those beliefs about yourself and your place in the world that benefit you, that promote emotional wellness. As such, rational beliefs lead to rational, emotionally healthy thoughts, which can in turn guide you toward seeking closure that is beneficial and healthy.

Not sure what your rational beliefs are? Here are some questions to ask yourself:

- When I envision my best self, what do I look like?
- As my best self, what am I contributing to the world around me? At home? At work? In my community?
- How do I feel when I am acting out of my best self? What is the evidence?
- How do other people react to me and treat me when I am at my best?
- When I am feeling at my best, what thoughts do I have that lead to these feelings?
- How am I benefiting the people in my life? What is the evidence?
- And what are the beliefs behind these thoughts?

Take some time and make a list of your rational beliefs. These are the guiding principles in your life, the foundation of who you want to be in the world and how you want others to treat you.

To help you along in creating your list of rational beliefs, here are some examples of rational beliefs that I have identified with my clients:

- The world is a safe place.
- Sometimes life goes the way I want it to, sometimes not, but I am not doomed to failure and unhappiness.
- I am kind to other people and I deserve the same in return.
- I have a right to ask for what I need.
- Some people will like me, others won't, but I am still a likable person.
- I am not always going to be understood by others, and I may not always understand them.
- I am not in control of how other people think, feel, or behave.

Keep your list handy. Add to it as you identify additional rational beliefs. Refer to this list when you find yourself in a situation in which you are sensing a need for closure and are forming, or questioning, your intentionality.

Closing Thought:
The Triumph and the Tyranny of Hindsight

It's human nature to spend a lot of time, often too much time, looking in the rearview mirror of life. Remembering, reviewing, reacting. Maybe rehearsing how we would act, what we would say, if we had the opportunity to do it all over again. As you evaluate how your attempt at closure went, remember that we can learn a lot by looking back if we're able to look at the past more objectively and learn lessons to carry forward. But so often we just end up judging ourselves and making ourselves feel more miserable.

I hope that if you sought closure, you got your desired, ideal outcome. But maybe you got closure that wasn't ideal, that answered your questions but in a way that made you sad or angry. Maybe you didn't get closure at all.

Here's what I often say to my clients: We do the best we can at the time with what we know and the resources we have available, including our own inner resources. What you bring to life in the present you may not have had access to when you sought closure—in fact, the process of trying to get closure may be what taught you the relevant lessons and helped you to become more self-aware. Again, you did the best you could at the time, and if you acted with intentionality and honesty, you probably did a pretty great job. We are all works in progress, often navigating the path between hope and despair. So show yourself some compassion.

Part IV
When You Don't Get the Closure You Want

Chapter 11

When to Walk Away

I hope that the methods we covered in part 3 help you find the closure you're looking for in a healthy and productive way. Hopefully you have an open and intentional conversation that ties up those loose ends for you, and you're able to move forward with your life in peace. However, as I've mentioned many times throughout this book so far, closure isn't always possible, for a variety of reasons.

This means sometimes you have to ask yourself the following question: Is it time to get on with your life *without* getting closure?

At this point, you may be thinking something like, "You've been telling me all about why I want closure and how to get it! Now you're telling me to forget about it and walk away?"

Well, yes.

That may sound harsh. I certainly don't mean it to be. However, holding out for something that remains out of reach, obsessing about it, and allowing it to play an outsize role in your life is just setting yourself up for unhappiness. Demanding closure when it's not forthcoming is essentially digging in and waiting for another person or entity to provide the healing you need—and being willing to sit in unhappiness until they do.

But as I mentioned in chapter 2, there's an alternative to closure, and that is acceptance. Whereas closure answers questions and resolves ambiguities, acceptance, well, *accepts* things as they are and moves on regardless. With acceptance, you may never get that sense of finality or understand *why* certain things happened as they did, but you nonetheless decide to let go of it, stop pursuing it, and focus on moving forward with your life. It doesn't sound as exciting as wrapping everything up in a neat package with a bow on top, but when closure is impossible, as it often is, acceptance is usually the best course of action.

I have up until now been focused on the emotional benefits of seeking and finding closure, as well as the emotional risks of not finding closure. In part 4 of this book, we will move in a new direction: what to do when you don't or can't get closure, starting with this chapter, in which we'll explore when to walk away and why.

Valuing Your Own Emotional Wellness

The decision to stop seeking closure in a given situation is one of the hardest decisions I see clients make. We all know how difficult it is, for all the reasons I discussed in part 2. Wanting to be right. Wanting to give or receive an apology. Wanting to feel in control. Wanting the other person to finally know how angry or hurt you are. And so on. But when an unsuccessful quest for closure is damaging your overall wellness, it can be worth the challenge to walk away.

"Walk away?" you may be asking. "You mean, give up on getting the closure I need?"

Let me answer that question with some more questions: How

much do you value your mental health? Your self-esteem? Your quality of life? In other words, how much do you value your wellness? I suspect on an average day you would say you value these things highly. Of course! Yet when I see the pain my clients are in because they can't or won't let go of their desire for closure, in my mind I'm wondering if that's really true.

I might not get much of a response beyond a shoulder shrug the first time I ask a client questions like these. Over time, however, the question of whether insisting on closure places their emotional wellness at risk often begins to take on new meaning.

As you're probably already aware, to at least some degree, body, mind, and spirit work together. Your emotional wellness has an effect on your physical wellness, and vice versa. If you have a stressful day at work, you might get a headache or break out in hives. Conversely, if you achieve a goal you've been working toward and you feel proud and happy, you might sleep well that night. And if you experience a string of disappointments—say, trying and failing to find closure over and over—you might find that your mood drops into the cellar, you don't have any energy, and you feel like your whole life is broken.

My focus as a mental health professional is on emotions, but I also see the effect that my clients' emotional states have on other areas of their lives. Over time, an unfulfilled need for closure can become detrimental to your emotional wellness and, consequently, to your overall wellness. This is why it's so important to learn how to evaluate when it's time to give up on closure and choose acceptance instead.

Let's look at some of the key indicators that it's time to walk away from closure for the sake of your own wellness.

Closure Has Become All-or-Nothing

One sign your attempts at closure are becoming unhealthy is that you've started seeing closure in all-or-nothing terms, feeling that if you don't get exactly what you're looking for, nothing about your life will be okay.

"If I don't get closure, I will . . ." The ways I most often hear clients end this sentence include: "be devastated," "never recover," "feel like a failure," "never rest," "just die." When I hear closure being described in terms of extremes, with the only options being getting what you want or total emotional collapse, an alarm goes off in my mind. I worry that my client is so invested in getting closure that they have essentially staked their emotional wellness on something that may be impossible to achieve.

Your mind can conjure up all kinds of reasons why you *must* have closure: you've suffered enough, you deserve it, and so on. That all may very well be true, but telling the world, the universe, or God what you absolutely *must* have is setting yourself up for a fall. The either-or dichotomy all too often falls into "or" territory. And where will that leave you?

The truth is that your life will not end if you don't get the closure you want, and if you feel like it will, that's a sign to take a step back and reevaluate whether it's time to walk away.

Closure Is All You Think About

We talk a lot about rumination in the mental health field. Rumination means tossing something around in your mind over and over, long past the point where that's healthy or productive, over-analyzing it from every different angle, imagining what you could have said or done differently and what the alternative outcomes might have been. This often means rehearsing a conversation (or confrontation), imagining what you'll say, and plotting all your comebacks, down to the final zinger that drives it all home. Every spare second, along with some seconds you can't actually spare, is spent fantasizing about the big moment that will give you the closure you want, need, deserve.

When you're fixated on something in this way, it seems like

everything you encounter triggers another memory, more thoughts about your fixation, and all the associated feelings. You're stuck in a maze, and every turn seems to lead you to the same dead end. Closure can feel like your only way out. Your salvation. In the absence of closure, you fall back into the obsessive rumination. No forward movement, no real satisfaction, no joy. Not until . . .

If this is your mental state, it's time to start looking at a different route out of the maze.

Closure Is All You Talk About

If you're thinking about closure obsessively, there's a good chance you're talking about it obsessively too. You're telling the same story to everyone who will hold still long enough to hear you out. The story about what you experienced, about how you tried to get closure, or how you want to try to get closure. Maybe you want some empathy. ("Haven't you felt this way too?") Maybe you want some sympathy. ("Don't you feel sorry for me?") Maybe you're looking for advice. ("What would you do in my place?") Whatever form it takes, you just can't stop talking about it. You're feeling bitter. You're dragging yourself down. You're dragging other people down. Getting closure has become your one and only purpose in life.

I'm reminded of a client who was hit by a cab driver while he was on a walk at dusk. He had stepped off the sidewalk to get around the slow walkers in front of him and all of a sudden found himself flying through the air. He broke some bones, and his injuries required staples and screws and lots of physical therapy. Every time we met, this client wanted to talk about that cab driver who wasn't paying enough attention, who he said ruined his life, whose only concern was not being blamed. My client wanted an apology. He wanted to know the cab driver hadn't had a moment's peace since the accident. He wanted more money from the settlement. He wanted closure on his terms. He exuded anger and bitterness to the point that his friends started avoiding him. It became the sole focus of his life, and wow, was he ever unhappy.

Now, those feelings were very understandable, but was his quest for closure actually bringing him toward peace and contentment, or was it pushing him further away?

You're Swimming in the Poison of Anger

Anger is a normal human emotion. When someone harms us in some way, we feel anger, and that's not always a bad thing. The problem arises when anger settles into our minds and begins to dominate all our thoughts and feelings. Closure, as discussed in chapter 4, can feel like the only way to release pent-up anger, and if we can't get the closure that we think will free us from our anger, we tend to get even angrier.

Unrelenting anger or rage can lead us to seek closure by trying to harm the other person, emotionally or in other ways. Anger can also cause us to avoid seeking closure because we just feel so justified and righteous as we wallow in all that anger—or, conversely, because we don't feel we deserve anything more than sitting in anger and resentment.

Not only is this kind of thinking potentially harmful for you and for the other person, but also it is based on the faulty assumption that we don't have the mental or emotional resources to manage our own anger, that we have to rely on someone else to give us closure if the anger is ever going to go away. This is untrue, and we can come to a state of acceptance all on our own, as I'll discuss in more detail in the next chapter.

You're Avoiding Grief

When we lose someone, through death, a breakup, or any other reason, we go through a grief process—letting go of the person we lost, feeling the accompanying feelings, integrating the loss into our minds, and starting a new chapter. Having closure with that person, however we define it, can help us say goodbye to them. Closure helps us to grieve.

But sometimes, especially with a death, the closure we want is impossible. We'll never get to say the things we want to say or hear the things we want to hear. Not getting that closure can make the grief process more difficult—so difficult, in fact, that you can become fixated on finding that closure. Rumination. Rehearsal. Demanding that God or the universe somehow provide you the closure you know you must have before you can move on.

After a loss, closure as you imagine it in your mind can essentially be magical thinking. Not real, not realistic, not possible. Grief is a process of gradually letting go. Demanding closure can prevent the grief process from even beginning. It can be a form of denial, an effort to avoid feeling the pain of grief, but in the end, it only results in your own prolonged suffering.

That's a sign it's time to walk away. (And remember, if grief or any other emotion becomes overwhelming, don't be afraid to reach out to a mental health professional. We are trained to be objective, nonjudgmental listeners, and we can help you sort out your feelings and learn coping techniques.)

SELF-ASSESSMENT: IS MY EMOTIONAL WELLNESS AT RISK?

The following are some questions that you may want to ask yourself as you assess your emotional health and consider the possibility of walking away from your own need for finding closure.

- Do I find myself frequently dwelling on what happened, reviewing actions and conversations?

- Do I rehearse multiple versions of the conversation I want to have with the person I want closure from?
- Do I feel like I can't ever be happy if I don't find closure?
- Has life begun to feel meaningless, like a treadmill that I must stay on until I find meaning through closure?
- Am I waiting for closure before I can allow myself to begin to process and accept a loss?
- Is my lack of closure leaving me with so much anger that I am frequently ready to blow up?
- Does what I experienced and my need for closure find its way into virtually every conversation?
- Do I feel like I'm having an existential temper tantrum, kicking and screaming to demand closure from the universe?
- Do I find myself saying, "Once I find closure, I can finally _____"?
- Do I sometimes or often feel like getting closure has become my only purpose in life?
- And finally: Is my need for closure getting in the way of being an optimistic, contented, productive person, involved in life, with loving relationships?

Beware of the Bully

In addition to prioritizing your wellness, another very good reason to stop seeking closure from someone is if they're bullying you or otherwise treating you badly. This can happen in a variety of ways, but the two I talk about most often with my clients are gaslighting and turning a conversation into a debate.

First: gaslighting. Gaslighting is when someone tells you something is just in your imagination in order to make you doubt yourself and your perceptions. (The term comes from the 1938 play *Gas Light*, in which a husband tries to make his wife think she's losing her mind by, among other things, gradually dimming the gaslights in their home and telling her she's imagining it.) It is a common tactic of someone who is in denial, who doesn't want to look at themselves. You'll hear a gaslighter say things like:

- "I didn't do that. Why would you say that?"
- "Don't you think you might be imagining this?"
- "That never happened. You're always so overdramatic."

Being gaslighted can be extremely frustrating, especially when it comes from someone you're trying to seek closure with. When you're running up against the wall put up by a gaslighter, you'll likely find yourself either becoming obsessed with proving yourself or wearied from hearing the same patronizing arguments. Either way, someone who gaslights you is going to stick to their story, and each time you hear it, you'll feel more disempowered. That means it's a good time to walk away.

Another cause of disempowerment is trying to have a conversation with someone who is intent on turning it into an argument. Some of us are more verbally adept than others, and trying to have a closure conversation with someone who wields their verbal adeptness like a weapon can be a real challenge. Instead of listening with an open mind, the other person argues with every point you make as a way of evading personal responsibility and possibly even intimidating you. I have had clients express shock at how their sincere attempts at closure were basically taken as an opportunity for a debate with the goal of proving them wrong.

When you're in this situation, you have a choice. You can lick your wounds and craft what you hope is an equally verbally adept second round (good luck with that!) or you can decide not to submit yourself to further abuse from someone who's only going to keep causing you harm. As your parents might have told you, the best way to deal with the playground bully is to choose not to engage. Walking away from someone who is an expert at verbal warfare is an act of empowerment.

The True Meaning of Compassion

One of the things that often holds my clients back from choosing acceptance over closure is concern that the other person "needs" them in some way or that they have to keep seeking closure to be a "good person." I sense this may be going on when I hear them say things like:

- "He's troubled. I know he doesn't mean it."
- "I can't abandon her. One day she'll realize how much she needs me."
- "They're stubborn. But I'll break down the wall if I keep trying."

Using this logic with yourself can be a way of keeping yourself stuck, of beating your head against a wall. You may be thinking, "But, Gary, I'm a compassionate person! This is an act of kindness! I'm willing to do whatever it takes to help this person realize that we need to find closure and repair our relationship. I'm the strong one. I can do this. They need my help."

Let me tell you my definition of compassion. Compassion means loving, respecting, and esteeming others and yourself. It does not mean enabling the bad behavior of the other person, allowing them to ignore or harm you, or sacrificing your own well-being in an attempt to help or fix them. That version of "compassion" doesn't benefit the other person, and it sure doesn't benefit you.

If you find that you're continuing to seek closure because

you think it's what a kind, compassionate person would do, even though it's going nowhere and causing you pain and suffering, that's a strong sign that it's time to walk away.

Other Reasons to Stop Seeking Closure

There are many other reasons why you might decide that your best course of action is to stop seeking closure and work on accepting the situation for what it is instead. Let's look at a few of the most common ones.

The Risk Is Not Worth the Potential Reward

If you're seeking closure with someone who has a history of being difficult, withholding, or outright abusive, the risk of the harm you may incur while seeking closure may not be worth the potential reward of gaining closure. If closure is a long, protracted process full of repeated meetings or even legal action that will further disrupt your life and/or cause you emotional harm, you may choose to place your energy elsewhere. Sure, you may gain the closure you wanted, but what will you have lost in the process, starting with your peace of mind? And what could you have gained, and avoided, through acceptance?

Questioning Your Own Motives

We've talked extensively about the importance of intentionality. As you consider your intentions for seeking closure, you may ask yourself some hard questions and consequently decide that seeking closure is not in your best interest. You may decide what you really want is to be proven right, or to receive an apology, or to get revenge. In some cases, on further consideration you might decide the issue is not as important to you as it once was, now that you're beyond the initial emotions. When you take an objective look at your intentions, and take the time to be clear with yourself, you may find yourself just as satisfied with the shoulder shrug of acceptance.

Seeking Closure May Damage the Other Person or Your Relationship

If you've ever been in the position of "telling someone off" and watching them crumble as a result of your words, then you know exactly why acceptance can be the best route to take sometimes. Sometimes people don't do what they should be doing—in romantic relationships, in friendships, in families, at work, in life—but it is the best they can do. Sure, they haven't been the person you needed them to be. But is closure going to get you what you want? And if it does, will their emotions, or their self-esteem, be collateral damage? Will your relationship survive? As the saying goes, while life isn't a war, it's still a good idea to choose your battles. Acceptance may benefit you both.

You Recognize the Other Person Won't Give You Closure

Throughout the previous chapters, I've discussed the many ways in which your request for closure may be met with a wall. You did your homework, your intentions were clear (at least to you), and you thought through how you wanted to approach someone to talk about closure. And yet the conversation went nowhere. The nonverbal attempts at closure I've discussed, such as acts of kindness and written messages, have been ignored. When do you decide to walk away? It's your choice, but when you find yourself in this situation, you may find that acceptance is ultimately your healthiest option.

Dodging Weaponized Closure

A reminder: closure can be used as a weapon. Someone who says they are seeking closure may not be doing so with intentionality. They may even be outright dishonest about wanting closure. A closure conversation with a person like this may ultimately be nothing more than a way to remind you of past harm, a way to reassert power over you, a way to set you up for more pain. When you accept the past and choose to move on, you become immune to attempts to pull you back into the past under the guise of closure. Armed with acceptance, you're able to recognize the wolf in sheep's clothing and walk (or run) away.

Listen to Your Gut

If at this point you're still asking, "How will I know when it's time to pull the plug on my attempts at closure and walk away?" there's a simple answer: listen to your gut.

It has been my experience that your instinct, your "gut," can be relied upon when you have a decision to make about how you're being treated by another person. I often ask my clients what their intuition is telling them about a situation they're in, and they frequently describe the little voice inside of them that's telling them what they need to do. Now, they may not want to listen to that voice. They may be actively talking themselves out of listening to it, coming up with all kinds of reasons why they should stay the course. But over time, your intuition may cause you to question your actions more and more. Lean into the discomfort, and listen for the lesson.

That small but persistent inner voice is always with us. It seldom leads us in the wrong direction. And even if you're hesitant to follow your instincts, they are certainly an important data point to consider as you make decisions.

The Process of Walking Away

So what do we do when we keep hitting a wall? Let's consider the process of walking away by looking at an example.

Saeed and Aria had been dating for a year, when Aria ended
their relationship abruptly with a text message. Saeed was heart-
broken and confused, and naturally he wanted closure. He and
Aria made plans to meet and talk, but when the day came, she
didn't show up. When he texted her to ask what happened, she
said she was busy and forgot. Saeed has sent two more texts asking
to find some time for them to meet, but Aria has stopped respond-
ing altogether.

What options is Saeed left with at this point? What comes next?

If Saeed were my client, we would probably start by discussing
the reasons he wants closure. I would talk to him about why he
wants to sit down with Aria. Is it to blow up at her? To try to hurt
her the way she hurt him? Or to talk about what happened in their
relationship and why Aria suddenly chose to walk away? What
questions does he hope to answer with a conversation like this?
(Common examples include "Why did this happen?" and "What,
if anything, did I do wrong?") Does he want her to know how bad
he feels, and does he want to hear how she feels? Does he want to
see if they can get back together or find a way forward as friends,
or is he hoping this will be the last time they speak?

I would also ask Saeed how he's feeling after being ghosted by
Aria. Without wasting too much time trying to figure out Aria's
motivations, is this surprising behavior or not, given what he
knows about her? Are his repeated requests for closure making
him feel better or worse? More empowered or less empowered?

I might ask Saeed about his fears. Is he afraid of what his
weekends will be like without Aria? Is he worried about how he'll
spend his time and who will be in his social circle? He might be
afraid of jumping back into the dating pool. He might be afraid
that he's not a lovable person and that he needs Aria to reassure
him of his lovability, something he feels he can't do for himself.
Asking yourself to name your fears can be scary, but it can also
open the door to becoming empowered.

It would also be important to discuss the power of engaging rational mind and taking a realistic look at the evidence. How has Aria responded to Saeed's requests—which were on their way to becoming pleas—to meet up? Was she saying yes and showing up? Was she saying "maybe" or "not right now"? Evidence speaks for itself, and if Saeed took a rational look at the evidence after coming to terms with his hopes and fears, he would likely conclude that Aria didn't want to have this conversation for whatever reason, and that he couldn't make her do so.

My goal would be to help Saeed understand his own heart and mind and to decide when it was time to walk away from seeking closure with Aria. And once he made that choice, it would be time to start setting limits with himself.

It has been my experience that when you want something that your rational mind tells you you're most likely not going to get, then it's time to set limits with yourself. For Saeed, that might mean stopping the texts to Aria and reminding himself that if there's going to be a next step, she has to be the one to take it. It might also mean unfollowing Aria on social media and asking mutual friends not to update him on her life. Setting limits for Saeed would also most likely mean getting more active in his life, finding new ways to spend his time, and building or rebuilding his friendship circle. Setting limits with yourself is a way to escape from the trap of disempowerment and find a pathway to empowerment.

EXERCISE:
VISUALIZE YOUR FREEDOM AND
YOUR PEACE OF MIND

Find a quiet place, free from distractions and noise. Get into a comfortable position. Close your eyes. Think of a current or past situation in which you needed closure but did not find it. Now visualize yourself facing the person who caused you pain. Rather than saying anything, give them a wave and then turn your back. Walk away from them toward a place that makes you happy, such as your home or the beach. Feel the feelings that come up as you walk. When you feel anger, sadness, or disappointment, consciously replace that feeling with other feelings, like relief, happiness, or just contentment. Say these words to yourself as you replace the old feelings with new ones: I accept. I let go. I learn. I move on.

You might want to do this exercise a few times or more—every time the need for closure finds its way into your thoughts, every time the old feelings come up. This visualization can help you make the decision about whether it's time to walk away. It can also help affirm your decision to walk away by reminding you that the past is behind you and the future is in front of you.

Closing Thought: Choosing You

The overarching message in this chapter is to make yourself a priority—specifically, to make your emotional wellness a priority. Our families and communities don't always teach us to do that. Instead, we are often taught that feelings are dangerous or a sign of weakness, and should thus be swallowed and denied. Many of us have not been taught to cope with uncomfortable or difficult feelings. Many of us have also been taught that other people cause our feelings and that it is up to the people who caused our feelings to take those feelings away.

Closure can be a very positive way to heal ourselves and our relationships. But seeking closure can also be a trip to nowhere, leaving us emotionally unwell and depleted. Only you know when it's time to walk away. How do you know? Listen to your inner intuition. Engage your rational mind. And ask yourself if continuing an uphill climb toward closure that you know in your heart is out of reach is worth the cost to your emotional wellness. If the answer is no, then it's time to walk away.

Chapter 12

Embracing Acceptance

At this point, we've identified the value of seeking closure and how it can heal individuals and relationships. But we've also identified the ways in which the pursuit of closure can be, for lack of a better term, a fool's errand, disempowering and emotionally self-destructive. So if closure proves impossible, where does that leave us? Continually feeling wounded, forced to move on when our hearts are broken, permanently frustrated, angry, and confused? Not quite. Not if we embrace acceptance.

As I was writing this chapter, I happened to hear a news story on the radio about two actors filing a lawsuit against a movie studio they said had wronged them more than fifty years ago. As a result of recent legislation, they were entitled to bring these charges to court, and they were seeking an astronomical amount of money. The reporter commented that, though they were now around seventy years of age, the two actors may finally find closure. For obvious reasons, this caught my interest.

As I considered their story, I agreed that they had been wronged. It seemed clear that they had not been treated with respect during their youth, a time when they didn't know how to protect themselves. But I also had to consider what this lawsuit would mean for them. Most likely there would be years of litigation filled with legal meetings and courtroom appearances, years that they might otherwise spend enjoying their lives with family and friends. Their past and present would be combed through, bringing to light private details they might not have wanted in the media, and possibly exposing them to cruel speculation, pity, or ridicule. Not to mention the potential loss of income they might incur while they chased after a settlement that might not add up to much after attorney fees.

But above all, I had to ask if prevailing in court would truly give them closure. A financial settlement might be enough to benefit them and their heirs. They might receive an apology from the studio or bring awareness to the plight of other young people in their situation. But would a check erase the pain they had experienced over the years . . . or would dredging up what happened to them mean reliving and even compounding the pain? Would winning the case finally give them the career success they said they'd missed out on as a result of their mistreatment? I had to wonder if all the time in court and all the negativity they'd have to endure to reach their victory, if they even won, would be worth it to reach the closure they were seeking. Or might it be, on balance, an empty victory when the benefit was weighed against the costs?

Then I considered the case from the perspective of acceptance. I'm not saying what happened to the two actors was right—not at all. But I had to wonder if they might have benefited from accepting the reality of what happened, for better and for worse. That wouldn't mean pretending the events of the past had no effect on them. An active acceptance could translate into action such as creating media awareness, raising funds, or creating a foundation to support and advocate for young people. Would this have brought them closure? And would it have been a more valuable form of closure for them, if it raised their spirits and connected them to humanity in a way that a lawsuit would not? This would require walking away from their concept of closure in the form of a big check. And it would require acceptance that what happened, happened.

In the last chapter, I discussed how to decide when it's time to give up on the pursuit of closure and turn instead to acceptance. In this chapter, we'll explore the benefits of embracing acceptance, as hard as it might initially seem.

Acceptance Is Power

It may seem counterintuitive, but acceptance is power. When I have this discussion with my clients, I am often met with resistance. They fear that if they stop seeking closure, they will be perceived as weak, emotionally unstable, unprincipled. They might see it as not standing up for themselves, not advocating for themselves, even cowering before a bully. And I totally understand that resistance. How can giving up on something and not getting what you want be a form of power? Let me explain.

We humans tend to get in our own way. We do that because of the ego. The ego wants to win, to be right, to prevail. The ego causes us to view situations from the perspective of good versus evil, with us as the good guy fighting against the bad guy. Our egos push us to engage so that we can prove ourselves superior, so that we can be the winner. The ego must be satisfied! I have often talked with clients who were seeking closure and hitting a wall but going back again and again out of their own need for ego satisfaction. On the other side of the issue, I have also all too often witnessed how the need for ego satisfaction can lead to withholding closure from someone who is seeking it, even when it might be beneficial to the relationship.

Here's a paradox for you: While your ego makes you desperately want to be powerful and in control, following your ego's demands often leads to out-of-control actions and feelings of powerlessness. It can cause you to stay in the game long after the signs clearly say it's time to walk away, because you equate walking away with defeat and can't imagine allowing yourself to be defeated. We become so obsessed with winning that we don't realize we've already lost.

Now, egos aren't all bad. A healthy ego can protect you from the futility of seeking closure that is not possible. It can guide you to recognize when it's time to walk away and help you to do so with your head held high. It can help you stop demanding closure that isn't worth pursuing or even needed. But a healthy ego is not based on feelings of superiority and dominance. It's based on owning that you are worthy—of love, of being treated with kindness and respect, of making choices in life that give you peace of mind, not further despair. And it's based on willingness to give this same consideration to others.

This is why, although it often seems like it at first, choosing acceptance over closure is not a sign of weakness. In fact, it takes a lot of strength to bring yourself to walk away from closure and to make your own peace of mind a priority, such that you choose not to submit yourself to further frustration, disappointment, anger, or abuse by attempting to drink from a well you've realized is empty.

When we fight for control over things we can't control (which is most things), we set ourselves up for failure and frustration. When we give up that fight, we open ourselves up to a whole new way of living. Acceptance means giving up the fight. No longer expecting what we can't rationally expect. Choosing to let go and move on, as hard as that may be when you're caught up in all the emotions that cause us to want closure. Accepting what we can't control in life frees us up to focus on what we *can* control. What a relief!

Walking away can mean taking back the power you have given away or finding a new awareness of your power, finally saying to yourself: "I don't need this person's understanding. I don't need their respect. I don't need their apology." Coming to this realization can open you up to how your personal power lives within you, emanating from you to the outside world. It is granted to you. You don't have to ask for it. You don't have to say, "Pretty please." You don't have to persuade or force someone else to give it to you. You own it.

Acceptance Is Rational

Choosing to walk away from the closure you were pursuing can be incredibly difficult when your thoughts and emotions are screaming at you that you simply *have* to get closure or you can't go on. This is where rational mind comes to your rescue. Rational mind allows you to objectively look at your thoughts and the feelings that arise from your thoughts, and to decide what's best for your own emotional wellness. Rational mind helps you to rise above the fray, to consider what you want from closure in a perfect world, and then to consider what's possible in the real world. Rational mind is the foundation for acceptance, for making choices in favor of your own emotional wellness, your own peace of mind, your own self-respect. When closure is not possible, acceptance is a rational choice.

Let me tell you a story about Jamal and Tim. Jamal was dealing with the very difficult breakup of a ten-year relationship. He described his ex-partner, Tim, as emotionally unavailable, present for the good times but not able to deal with the hard stuff, not very emotionally supportive, and quick to avoid uncomfortable

discussions. At first, he tried to talk through these issues and save
the relationship, but he was met with denial from Tim: "I don't see
a problem. What's the problem?" Jamal finally decided he couldn't
count on him for the long haul and decided to cut his losses. He
drove the point home by finding an apartment and moving out on
his own.

Tim was angry when Jamal moved out. Jamal wanted Tim to
know why he had made this choice—how hard he had tried, how
he felt he was never quite there for him—but when he tried to text
him, Tim ignored him. Jamal called, and Tim told Jamal that when
he was ready to apologize and make amends, they could meet and
talk. Jamal felt that he had no reason to apologize and that getting
together under those circumstances would only lead to a repeat of
what he had been going through for ten years. Jamal tried again
to see if they could have a conversation and was given the same
ultimatum.

"I know what you must be thinking," Jamal said to me. "It is
what it is." He rolled his eyes. "I've been saying it to myself. It's a
tired cliché, but it sure fits in my case. I wanted closure. I thought it
would help me to move forward with my life. I thought it would
help us both. But I have to recognize that I'm not going to get
closure, as much as I think I deserve it. I have to accept that."

I asked Jamal how I could support him in coming to accep-
tance.

"Actually, I started that process myself, I'm proud to say. I
looked in the mirror this morning, and I said to myself: 'Jamal, let
go of it. Let it be.'"

Of course, some part of Jamal still wanted a nice, satisfying
closure conversation—or any conversation at all. But by using his
rational mind, he was able to recognize that it wasn't going to
happen and to stop pursuing it.

EXERCISE:
LET IT BE

You might agree, based on your own experiences, that the words "let it be" can be magical, and not only because of the beautiful Beatles song. Letting it be is about giving up control of what you can't control and freeing yourself up to focus on what you can control. Take some time to think about what acceptance means to you personally. Go off by yourself with a sheet of paper. Say the words "let it be." What comes to mind? Write it down. Say it again. Write your response again. Open up your mind and consider all aspects of your life. What's going on at home where letting it be might benefit you or others? What about work? In your community? Do any loose ends come to mind that you've been aching to achieve closure on? Is it time to let it be?

Acceptance Is Compassion

Walking away from closure can help you to be a more compassionate person. How? Not getting what you want and feeling disempowered can make you intensely aware of your own suffering. If you're able to walk away from that suffering instead of continuing to subject yourself to it, it can be an opportunity to do some soul-searching. You may ask yourself questions like, "Why was this so important to me? What did I need so badly from this other person that I was willing to become disempowered? Maybe I didn't need it at all." Your answer may open the door to a greater level of self-acceptance.

This can motivate you to take better care of yourself, to be kinder to yourself. It is incredibly empowering to show yourself compassion. To let yourself be who you are without shame. To not feel the need to apologize for being yourself. To accept your own imperfections and your own gifts. In short, to say yes to yourself!

Furthermore, when you become aware of what lies beneath your own suffering, you have the unique opportunity to be aware of the suffering of others and maybe want to show them more kindness. If your unsuccessful attempt to get closure with someone helped you to recognize the damage they've sustained in life (or the pain they experienced as a result of your attempt at closure), you might be even more in touch with your compassionate side. Compassion is an inside-out job; if you're compassionate toward yourself, you are more likely to show compassion toward others.

Learning Life's Lessons

Ideally, we like to think that achieving closure will bring a new sense of self, improve our self-esteem, increase our ability to speak up and demand what we deserve. Sometimes closure does indeed do that. We feel empowered, vindicated, understood. And that's a valuable life lesson.

But personal growth as a human requires being open to all the potential lessons that life can teach us, both those that can be celebrated and those that must be endured. Life gives us many challenges, leaving emotional bumps and bruises along the way, but in a way, those challenges are a gift, because they teach us lessons that help us grow as humans. And the gracious thing to do when offered a gift is to accept it. Some of my most important life lessons I have learned the hard way, through experience. I think that the experience of failing to get closure, hard as it may be, can yield valuable life lessons. The letter you sent and then later regretted sending, due to the damage it caused to the other person or to your reputation. The public snub that was returned in force and left you feeling exposed and humiliated. All of these can potentially teach us something.

One of the reasons I have emphasized the importance of intentionality is that it lets you get clear with yourself on why you need closure and what you're expecting from the other person, and to be okay with those responses. In the process of thinking through your intentionality, you may decide you're not ready emotionally, or that your desire for closure isn't realistic, or that you might potentially do emotional damage to the other person. In other words, you will learn something about yourself during this process—a life lesson.

Behind every life lesson is a story, so I'll tell you a story about Mark.

Mark grew up in a small town where everybody knew each other. His father ran a little diner, what Mark referred to as a "glorified hot dog stand," that never did very well. As a result, Mark's family lived close to the poverty line. They had a tiny house with one bedroom, which his parents slept in, while Mark and his older brother slept on cots in the living room. His parents worked long hours in the diner, leaving Mark and his brother to take care of themselves. On top of that, his parents often fought. His mother wanted their father to let go of the diner and find a higher-paying job of some kind. She said the diner was built on "a dollar and a dream, and we don't even have the dollar." His father always promised them business would pick up, but it never did.

Mark was ashamed of his family's situation. The kids at school made fun of his secondhand clothing. He never brought any of his friends home with him, but they all knew how he lived.

When Mark's brother graduated from high school, he immediately went into the military and cut ties with the family beyond an occasional phone call. Mark is barely in touch with him. Mark, meanwhile, went to a state university on a scholarship, finding summer employment on campus so that he wouldn't have to live at home again.

Mark is now thirty-two years old and works as a teacher in

another state. He sees his parents a couple of times a year; they still work long hours in the diner. He feels that it has taken him years to get past the damage of his childhood—the deprivation, the ridicule he endured, and his parents' obliviousness to how their choices, especially his father's, impacted their sons."

Last summer, Mark made a trip to his hometown to visit his parents for a weekend. (He got a room in a local hotel, as he couldn't bring himself to sleep on his old cot.) He had an intention in mind. He wanted to tell his parents how hard his life had been as a child, how the poverty resulting from their bad choices had affected him, how it drove his brother away. He wanted them to acknowledge how he had struggled to develop a sense of himself as a person, to not always feel less than everyone around him, to finally recognize that he was worthy of having more in life than he had as a child. Mark didn't expect an apology, didn't even want one. But he did want them to understand how he felt about what he saw as his father's selfishness and inability to face reality, as well as his mother's unwillingness to put her foot down and make a better life for her children.

But when Mark started to talk about his childhood, his father interrupted him and talked about the potential of the diner and how the community never supported him, how it could have been a great restaurant had he been given a chance. His mother told him what a great mother she had been, how she and her father had taught him and his brother solid values. They continually talked over him, returning to the same message of what could have been, what should have been. When he tried to tell them how unhappy he had been as a child, how he had felt like an outsider at school, his mother said to him: "Nonsense. You were a happy child. You loved playing at home with your brother while we worked. Don't you remember? I guess all that college education taught you to make your parents the bad guys."

"Okay," Mark said. "Okay, Mom and Dad." He didn't have the

heart or the energy to keep arguing, or the desire to hurt them. If they couldn't hear him and try to understand him, then he was wasting his breath.

He was somewhat surprised at his mother's defensiveness and his father's silence, but he was beginning to realize how invested his parents were in maintaining the story of this fictional happy childhood, in which he and his brother had everything they needed, materially and emotionally. They couldn't look at the mistakes they'd made, how they had wasted their lives on a diner that was never going to be successful. Acknowledging Mark's childhood unhappiness would mean taking responsibility for their own life choices. And if they did that, what would they have left? Instead, they gaslighted him, telling him his memories weren't real, that they were the product of too many psychology classes combined with the passing of time. They insisted he had forgotten the happy life they had given him and just needed to be reminded.

By accepting the reality of his parents' limitations, Mark was able to leave their home with a few valuable lessons that he could take with him back to his own life. One of the lessons was that his parents did the best they could with what they had. They hadn't done a great job as parents, or with their own lives, but they didn't have the resources—mental, emotional, financial—to do better. Another lesson Mark came away with was that not everyone, certainly not his parents, can look objectively at their own lives, for fear they might collapse under the burden of the truth. Perhaps most significantly, Mark also went home owning his power to control his own destiny, whether his parents approved or not. He realized that he'd had that power all along, that it was what had brought him to where he was now in life, but he hadn't yet really owned it. Now he could see it clearly and use it to its full potential.

Mark didn't get the closure he wanted with his parents, the closure he thought he needed. Instead, he uncovered valuable life lessons. That is the power of embracing acceptance.

Life Doesn't Always Make Sense

One of the main reasons we want closure in the first place is because we want things to make sense. We want to understand why someone acted as they did or why events unfolded in a certain way. Even if we don't like the answers, we still would rather hear them than hear no explanation at all. But the truth is that in the real world, things don't always make sense.

Consider everything in life that you take on faith because it doesn't necessarily make sense to you personally. If I had to make sense of everything I encounter in daily life, I wouldn't leave my home. It doesn't make sense to me how a skyscraper can be built from the ground up, but I still take the elevator to the twentieth floor. It doesn't make sense to me how the weather can change so quickly, but I still grab my umbrella when I need to. It doesn't always make sense to me why a client is so devastated by a conversation that seemed simple enough to me, but I still listen and give them emotional support as they find their way forward.

I frequently say to my clients, "People are who they are." That statement is met with a range of responses, from sad agreement, to shoulder shrugging, to blowing up, to statements like "Well, they shouldn't be!" Sure, in a perfect world, people "should be" better, but we don't live in a perfect world. I can speak for myself here: My life got a whole lot easier when I stopped expecting other people to act how I thought they should act and started accepting them on their own terms. Not demanding, not begging, not expecting sense. Just allowing them to be who they are. Life also got a whole lot easier when I stopped expecting life to be logical or fair. It's often neither.

Nearly every week I give this same advice to a client, and they often come back to me and say it was life-changing for them too. It doesn't mean we can't have expectations for our loved ones, but it does mean understanding that what they *can* give us is not always what we wish they *could* give us in a perfect world.

When you give up the demand that the world and its inhabitants make sense, you give yourself and everybody around you the space to be the messy humans we all are. You give them the grace to do their best, regardless of whether their best meets your own standards. Grace! Such a simple word, such a powerful word.

I have been conditioned, like many people have, to view a shrug of the shoulders in a negative way. A sign of not caring, laziness, or weakness. But when facing down your own expectations that another person give you closure by making sense, coming to the realization that it's time to shrug your shoulders and walk away can be a sign of strength, acceptance, power.

Tools for Embracing Acceptance

Now we come to the question of the hour: How do I embrace acceptance when my whole being is aching to find closure? The answer is simple and also hard. You walk away by deciding to walk away. If you're waiting to finally feel angry or frustrated enough, you're setting yourself up for more anger and frustration. If you're waiting to feel inspired or at peace, you might be waiting a very long time. Instead, you make a rational choice. You say to yourself, "I don't need to fight this battle anymore. A lot of life doesn't make sense, and this doesn't either. This is what I need to do for my own peace of mind, my own sense of self, my own personal power."

You have a choice here. You can take actions to make your emotional health a priority and, in the process, begin to feel whole again. Here are some tools to address your emotional wellness while letting go of the need for closure. If there's a theme here, I think it's to come to acceptance by embracing your life. Embrace it so hard that you don't have time to ruminate about what you didn't get, because you're so focused on what you do have.

Watch Your Self-Talk

Self-talk refers to the ongoing dialogue we carry on in our minds every waking moment. Our self-talk is often filled with judgment and criticism of ourselves and others. Replaying the woulda coulda shoulda tapes to ourselves only makes us more unhappy. But you can choose self-talk that is kind. You can give yourself permission to be human like everyone else, and you can reassure yourself that you are doing the best you can, also like everyone else.

Adopt an inner voice of compassion and kindness toward yourself. Speak to yourself as you would speak to a friend or family member who has been hurt by another person. Catch yourself when you slip into self-criticism, either/or thinking, declarations of how bleak your future looks, and so on. Remind yourself that life is essentially good and that there are a lot of people in the world who mean well, including many people in your own life.

Set Limits with Yourself

If you find yourself constantly dwelling on the closure you didn't achieve, you'll probably realize sooner or later that giving it constant attention is doing more harm than good. Sometimes we have to employ some tough love with ourselves and set limits on our own thoughts and actions.

Make a conscious decision to place your thoughts somewhere else, even temporarily. Make an effort to speak with friends and family about something other than the situation that has led to your need for closure. Avoid situations in which you're more likely to dwell on your need for closure, like staying in bed all morning on a weekend or sitting alone at a bar.

Keep reminding yourself that you walked away for a reason. Sure, you've gone over and over in your mind why you want closure and what you're giving up if you don't get it. But what about what you gain by letting go of the need for closure, such as having more space in your mind to think about the future, feeling calm and grounded, or being able to feel joy again? Stop the self-punishment. Replace it with kindness. You deserve it!

Distract Yourself

Positive distractions help you avoid dwelling in a dark place by purposefully engaging you in thoughts and activities that help you stay grounded, that bring pleasure, that connect you to your life. If you find yourself struggling with recurring thoughts and feelings about closure you have not been able to realize, choosing to focus on healthy distractions—hobbies, time with friends, your work—is a great way to engage with what brings you joy in your life and help you transcend the feelings that accompany not achieving closure, like frustration, disappointment, and anger. Positive distractions are little pieces of evidence that can add up to greater awareness that life is good.

Connect, or reconnect, with activities in your life that you enjoy. The idea is to move your energy away from thoughts about closure and the toxicity that may be associated with those thoughts by occupying your time in more positive or productive ways. Listening to music. Watching a movie. Taking a walk. Cooking. Exercising. (By the way, physical activity is a great way to get the endorphins flowing and help to counter negative emotions and stress.) If you start to move in this direction, you might also become more aware of what you have sacrificed in your life as a result of your desire for closure, which might make it easier to let go of that desire.

Expand Yourself

Closure is often about something that didn't go the way you wanted it to or that was taken away from you. So consider bringing something new into your life in its place. Find a new hobby. Take a class. Plan a trip. Do some volunteering.

Volunteering or performing other acts of kindness can be

especially helpful because it focuses your attention away from your own problems as you help someone else with theirs. You can help heal yourself of harm that was done to you by being intentional about healing harms done to others. Showing kindness is a way of affirming your own power by not allowing yourself to become embittered, caustic, defeated. It shows you refuse to be diminished by how others have treated you or the disappointments you have experienced.

Try Meditation

You might consider getting involved in a meditation or spiritual practice to give you additional tools to help you to heal. One of the most common and accessible is mindfulness meditation, which helps you stay in the moment instead of hovering between the two places where the human mind tends to get stuck: staring into the rearview mirror lamenting over the past, or gazing into the crystal ball and worrying about the future. Mindfulness meditation brings you into your life, fully aware of the here and now. Many people find it to be a big help in keeping calmer and more centered. If you're not sure where to start, there are many apps, websites, and books to help you get going.

Visioning is another technique somewhat similar to meditation that can help you with finding acceptance. Spend a few minutes in the morning or at night creating an image in your mind of parting ways with the person you were unable to achieve closure with. Not an angry vision but one in which you choose to walk away from them, maybe with a hug or handshake, maybe just turning and walking in a different direction. Creating this vision in your mind on a regular basis can help you feel a greater sense of acceptance over time.

Get Support

You may have found yourself isolating lately while you focus on your need for closure. Or you might have been spending a lot of time venting to friends and family, to the point where you're starting to wonder if they're avoiding you. Either way, choose to connect with the people you care about, and who care about you, in a new way. Initiate get-togethers and make it clear that you're moving on and want to talk about something new. Ask them more questions about themselves. Consider activities like a movie or a concert that involve being in each other's presence with less talking. Be willing to apologize if you sense they have grown weary of listening to you vent.

Embrace Your Rational Mind

Take a step back and observe your thoughts, and the feelings that result. Articulate for yourself any holes in your reasoning. In particular, take an honest look at what you were expecting in terms of closure and, given what you've experienced, what you can reasonably expect going forward. Remind yourself of the benefits of walking away from closure that is not realistic or possible.

Engaging your rational mind may be a process. Keeping a journal can help you to track your progress and move the process along. Sit down and write your thoughts about why you wanted closure, what you did to try to bring it about, what prevented you from reaching closure, and the lessons you learned. Be sure to consider what it means to come to acceptance, what it will mean going forward, and how you will benefit from it.

While you are engaging rational mind, also remind yourself that you have a choice. You can choose to think and behave in a rational manner. You can heal yourself.

SELF-ASSESSMENT:
WHAT'S GETTING IN THE WAY OF COMING TO ACCEPTANCE?

Does acceptance sound like an uphill climb? Here are some questions to ask yourself to assess your own readiness to accept:

- What thoughts come to mind when I consider the words "let it be"?
- What feelings do I experience when I have these thoughts?
- Can I accept what happened to me while also accepting that the other person behaved badly, or does acceptance feel like condoning how I was harmed?
- Am I so invested in making sure I have closure with the other person involved that acceptance feels like weakness?
- What am I giving up if I choose acceptance?
- What am I gaining if I choose acceptance?
- What are the emotional risks and other risks if I decide I can't accept what happened?
- What role is my ego playing in the decision to embrace acceptance?
- What would my life be like if I fully accepted that I can't have closure?
- How would acceptance contribute to my own personal growth?

Admittedly, these are hard questions, but doing the work here has the potential to greatly enhance your peace of mind and help you move forward with your life. You're worth the work.

Closing Thought:
The First Step toward Freedom

I know it's not easy to simply accept something that has caused you so much pain. You might be thinking, *How can I walk away and let this be?* But when you're hitting a wall, or you're risking being sucked into more abuse, or closure is impossible for any other reason, what is your alternative? People are who they are. We can't force them to be what we want them to be, even if only to make it easier to end a relationship.

Acceptance is not closure, and at first that may seem like a downside. It means there are certain loose ends that may never be tied up. But the fact that acceptance isn't closure also means it's not closure that you begged for from someone else, it's not closure that you achieved at someone else's expense, it's not closure that you didn't want but was forced upon you. Acceptance is something you do for yourself and by yourself. It is a rational, compassionate, empowering choice. It lets you get ready to take charge of your life and go forward with confidence. Acceptance is the first step toward freedom.

Chapter 13

Getting Closure After a Death

E very week, if not multiple times in a week, I speak with a
client about loss. When we experience any kind of a loss, we
experience grief. If we lose a friendship, we grieve that loss,
even if we decided at some point that this friendship was ulti-
mately not good for us. If we lose a job, we grieve the loss of the
income security it provided, the opportunity to be productive, or
the relationships we had with coworkers, even if we decided the
job was more pain than gain, even if we were pushed out or fired,
even if we left for a better job. We grieve the loss of a romantic
relationship, no matter who chose to end it, and we grieve the loss
of opportunities to really connect with family members due to
differences or disagreements we can't seem to overcome. In my
work with clients facing chronic and catastrophic health condi-
tions, I often talk with them about the grief they experience after
a medical diagnosis; they grieve for the life they had before their
diagnosis, and the future they believed they would have when life
was going according to plan until it suddenly wasn't.

And of course, when a loved one dies, we grieve. When I told friends and clients that I was writing a book about closure, many asked me if it was a book about grief after a loved one's death. Certainly, a death is far from the only reason why we might seek closure, but it is a particularly tricky one, both because of the intensity of the pain involved and because it is permanent in a way other closure-related situations usually aren't. So, while I have touched upon closure after losing a loved one throughout this book, I wanted to address it more specifically in a dedicated chapter.

Will Closure Make the Pain Go Away?

I have lost many people throughout my life, and I suspect you've experienced losses of your own. The death of a loved one leaves us with pain that is difficult to put into words. In my own experience, as well as the experiences of many of my clients, the pain of loss evolves over time. Grief looks different for everyone, and there is no right way to grieve, but it often starts with excruciating pain, the kind of emotional pain that makes you want to scream and cry and beat a pillow and kick a door. It's a pain that can make you think you're losing your mind. You feel like your insides are going to come out through your mouth. Your pain may feel so intense that you fear it will overtake you, that you will collapse under the weight. And you do collapse, maybe repeatedly. But somehow you keep going.

Over time, the excruciating pain begins to subside into a dull ache that pervades your thoughts, your actions. You wonder if you're walking more slowly, speaking more slowly. Life feels like it's in slow motion. You're surrounded by memories of this person. A song, a TV show, the smell of a certain food, a comment you hear . . . all trigger more memories. The dull pain threatens to become intense again. Sometimes it does, and you suddenly feel pain as fresh as the day they died.

When you're grieving, you struggle to admit your loved one won't be in your life ever again. Your rational mind tells you that you have to acknowledge they won't be back, but admitting they're gone can feel like giving up. You feel unsettled, disconnected. You try to smile, to appear upbeat, while looking at the world through a dark haze. You want to be at peace with their death, but you don't know how to find peace.

In conversations around grief, my clients often say things like: "How can I make this pain go away? It just hurts so much. It's overwhelming." "Will I ever feel happy again?" And of course: "How do I get closure?"

In training for grief counseling, we mental health professionals are taught to encourage our clients to talk and to feel. To talk about their feelings. To tell the story of the death if they choose to. To share memories. To talk about what their lives are like now that this person is gone. Each time the stories of loss are told, each time the feelings are experienced, the mind begins to integrate the loss. I believe in the power of talk and the potential of putting thoughts and feelings into words, but . . . what my grieving clients want is closure. They want to resolve those loose ends that torture them, that refuse to give them a moment of peace, that they believe must be the magic key to making all of this okay.

I know how they feel. When I have lost a loved one, I have caught myself begging the universe for just five more minutes. Just to see them one more time. To remind them how much I loved them and still do. Maybe to say words that I wanted to say but didn't. Maybe to ask for forgiveness for a time when I could have been kinder, more supportive, more loving, but wasn't. To get answers to questions, such as "Did you know how much I cared about you?" And maybe even to have them ask me for forgiveness too. My grieving clients have often expressed the same wishes.

Would that provide closure? Would it make the pain go away? Maybe, but I imagine the relief would be temporary, and the dull ache of grief would return. And in any case, it's impossible. So what kind of closure *would* help us feel better?

In helping clients through grief, I have heard a lot of stories about seeking closure as a way of resolving grief after a death, some more successful than others.

For example, I've had more than one client attempt to use the legal system as a way of achieving closure. I've met with parents who were devastated by a child's death that was the result of errors made by healthcare professionals. I've met with parents of young adults who were killed in a traffic accident involving a drunk driver. At times, our sessions became updates on meetings with their attorneys, progress reports as their case inched its way through the legal system. I watched these clients' faces contort in anger as they described meetings during which they felt they were being gaslighted, their pain minimized by the lawyers representing their opponents, who were generally large hospital systems and insurance companies. In these conversations with my grieving clients, they often expressed the same goal: "I will make them give me closure." Their anger energized them—for the moment. And then they fell back into the deep pit of their grief.

I'm not saying these people were wrong to take legal action. Depending on the situation, it can be important financially, or it can help prevent a person or institution from harming additional people in the future. But I don't think I ever saw it help my clients achieve emotional closure or process their grief. At the end of the day, they still lost someone they deeply loved.

Other clients have approached post-death closure in a different way, hoping for dreams in which their loved one would come to them and give them whatever reassurances and answers they needed. Or they hoped for a sign, like the client who found a dollar on the street, the amount of her weekly allowance as a child, and was sure it was a message from her mother. I had one especially memorable client who was so desperate to find closure after the loss of his partner that he made an appointment with a psychic medium who claimed to be able to speak to the dead. He described his goal in meeting with this medium as: "I need my partner to tell me he's still with me. That would give me closure."

On the more conventional side of things, our culture provides us with the means to gain closure through funerals, memorial services, or celebrations of life. These events often include a religious or spiritual message, eulogies, and informal sharing of thoughts and memories. I have been to many, as you may have also. A funeral can be a time to mourn together, to feel supported, and I think this can be helpful in moving toward some level of closure. However, going to an event honoring someone you loved and lost can also be a grueling emotional experience. Sure, there are lots of hugs and expressions of condolence, but they're accompanied by the hard smack in the face of reality that this person is no longer here, and you're being reminded of it by a roomful of people, some of whom you might not even really want to spend time with (and maybe a few your loved one wouldn't really have wanted to spend time with either). Words meant to provide closure, such as "They're in a better place" or "Time heals all wounds," just sound empty, in spite of the good intentions of the speaker.

We all need to do different things to cope with the loss of a loved one. No judgment. Grief is an individual journey for each of us, a journey we are forced to take every time we lose someone we love. I understand the need for closure and the hope behind seeking closure after a loss, the desperate need to heal the pain. The pain is so hard to sit with.

However, I see a theme here in these examples of seeking closure after a death. The theme is seeking closure through other people: the legal system, a psychic medium, an event, the hugs and condolences of loved ones. Seeking closure through the actions and words of other people, as I have discussed in previous chapters, is always a gamble. We may or may not receive the big payout from the insurance company. The sign we are seeking may or may not come. The funeral may or may not be the kumbaya moment our culture intends it to be. And even if those things happen, we might not feel the way we thought and hoped we'd feel.

I have to confess that I'm not sure if other people truly can give us closure when we're in the throes of grief. I'll take it a step further: I'm not sure if I even know what closure *is* after the death of a loved one. Reassurance that we were the person they needed us to be? Affirmation that they are off on their next journey, maybe waiting for us to join them someday? Forgiveness for the times we caused them pain? Or is closure having the pain of the loss taken away from us, replaced with peace, comfort, or joy?

The traditional rituals of closure after a death can provide us with a sense of support and community, and spiritual and religious beliefs can provide additional meaning when death doesn't seem to make any sense. However, when all is said and done, losing someone is like a big kick in the stomach. It leaves us gasping for air, confused, asking questions that are unanswerable. Life is random and unfair. People come into our lives, and we love them, and sometimes we lose them. And then we feel alone.

At least in theory your boss can tell you why she fired you. Your boyfriend can tell you why he broke up with you. Your sister can tell you why she stopped speaking to you. But death is forever. A loss leaves you with a wound. Closure, whatever that means for you, may offer you some measure of comfort, but it is not going to heal that wound.

The Grieving Process as a Form of Closure

I can say with conviction that the grieving process provides hope for navigating the journey of loss. I don't believe that grief unfolds in predetermined steps. I don't believe it is completed within a specific time frame. I don't believe it is predictable. What I do believe is that each person goes through grief in their own way. I also believe that each loss is unique; you might grieve one way when one person passes from your life, and a completely different way when another person passes.

The only guaranteed way to get through grief is to go through the process. To talk. To allow yourself to feel. To find personal ways to memorialize the person you lost. To share memories. To live your life in a way that carries on their legacy.

Each time we lose someone we love, we start a new chapter in our lives: the chapter without that person. This may mean big changes, such as when we lose a partner. It might mean smaller changes, such as when we lose a coworker or a friend. Either way, it means a new chapter. Something funny will happen, and you'll think of sharing the joke with the person you lost, only to remember you can't. A problem will arise, you'll need some advice, and they'll be the first person who comes to mind, until you realize they're not here to help you. Holidays and birthdays will come around, and you'll think of celebrating with them, but you can't anymore.

As we embark on this new chapter ahead, we can do so with an open heart, accepting that we carry that wound and choosing to walk with it, to soothe ourselves when we need to, but to keep walking. Going through your own grief process in this way is the closure you give yourself.

My Story: Dad, Mom, and Me

I started this book with a personal story in part 1, and now I'll close with one. My parents are no longer with me. At the end of my father's life and, ten years later, my mother's life, I came away with a lot of thoughts about closure after a loved one's death. I would like to share them with you.

My father and I were often not on the same page. I talk with a lot of men in my line of work, and I know this experience is not uncommon; many of us have had complicated relationships with our fathers. Mine was born in the 1920s, when many men were reared to express one single emotion, and that was anger. Many men of his generation were angry when they felt anger, and they often learned to be angry when they felt fear, disappointment, sadness. My father was angry a lot. Growing up with him wasn't always easy for me, and I suspect it wasn't easy for him. His bookish middle son was a mystery to him. He tried to be helpful to me in many ways, but he often communicated out of anger, and that was hard for me to understand as a child. Looking back on my childhood with the 20/20 vision of adulthood, I understand that, like most parents, he raised his children with what he knew. He did the best he could to be a father in spite of his own demons. But at the time, we were just not often on the same page.

After I left home and went out on my own, my father tried to bridge the gap between us, and I didn't always make the effort to meet him halfway. I had a lot of feelings about our relationship, and to try to talk about what had happened between us seemed too hard. I told myself that it would be too hard for *him*, but even at the time I knew that was an excuse for not wanting to talk about the past myself.

I had an image in my mind of a conversation I would one day have with my father. I wanted to tell him how I felt about growing up with him, how he helped me to grow up and how he didn't help. I wanted him to know why I behaved toward him as I did sometimes. I wanted to better understand why he often behaved toward me as he did. Most of all, I wanted us to forgive each other. Looking back, I realize now that what I wanted was closure with him.

As he got older and his health started failing, I became increasingly aware that my father's time was running out. Still, I thought there was time. I thought the opportunity would somehow magically present itself, like in the movies. I thought that we would find our closure before he passed.

One year, I went back to Michigan to visit my parents for what turned out to be my father's last Christmas. On Christmas Eve, I had the feeling he wanted to say something to me. I remember sitting across from him in the living room and having the thought that I should open this conversation with him. He was never great at saying what was on his mind. I could have started the conversation, but I didn't. Instead, I told myself that we would find a better time. Certainly better than Christmas Eve. And so I asked what he wanted to watch on TV, and the moment passed.

My father became very ill with the cancer we suspected he might have during the summer after that Christmas. When he and my mom came to visit me in New York City, he looked sick and moved and spoke very slowly, and we spent a lot of time sitting in the Midtown hotel room I had booked for them. One of my last memories of my father was our breakfast in the hotel restaurant the morning they left. He told me about a time when he was much younger and his company had sent him to New York City on a business trip for a couple of days. I had heard this story many times growing up, but I sensed he needed me to hear it again. And so I listened like it was the first time. I told him what an amazing experience that must have been, how valuable he must have been to his company. I think he needed my validation, to know that he was a father who had done things he could be proud of and that I could also be proud of. That he mattered in the world. I'm thankful I had the presence of mind to give it to him. Before he left New York to return to Michigan, he touched my shoulder and said, "Thanks for always listening to me." I answered, "You're welcome, Dad. Always."

A few months later, I came home to visit him while he was dying in the hospital. I knew we still needed to have this conversation, so one morning I got up very early to get to the hospital before my siblings and mom arrived. I walked into his room and saw that he had been heavily drugged to help him deal with the pain he was experiencing. He was out of it. I sat down and began crying, because I knew the moment for closure had passed, and the opportunity probably wouldn't return. And it didn't. Dad was never really coherent again.

That morning, he was mumbling in his sleep, moving around a little bit, agitated. I got up from my chair and stood next to him. I said, "Hi, Dad, I'm here." I put my hand on his shoulder and held it there. After a few moments, he stopped mumbling and became still. His sleep became more peaceful. I think he knew that everything was okay between us. I felt the same way, my hand on his shoulder, watching him at rest. I leaned down and gave him a kiss on the forehead.

That was the closure I got with my dad. It wasn't how I imagined it would be. The closure I really wanted was that Christmas Eve conversation, or the one I had hoped to have in the hospital. Instead, this was the closure we found. It wasn't enough, and I have had to accept that.

It was very different with my mom. She spent the last couple of years of her life with great difficulty in walking, essentially unable to care for herself. I spent one weekend a month with her during those two years, sitting for hours on end watching reruns of police procedurals. I would often take her for a drive to get us both some fresh air. We would drive through our old neighborhood, past where I went to school, or to the area where she grew up.

I realize now that my mom needed closure—not closure with me but rather closure on her life. She told me many stories about her childhood on our drives. How she grew up. What was done for her but also what was done to her, by adults who were supposed to watch over and care for her. These were stories I'd never heard before, and I'll be honest: part of me didn't want to hear most of them. I didn't want to have to think of the little girl who became my mother living in poverty, not having what she needed, being mistreated by authority figures, not having the opportunities that she and my father worked so hard to provide for my siblings and me. I cursed the teacher who wouldn't let a little girl eat what lunch her parents were able to provide because she couldn't understand an arithmetic problem. I blessed the farm owner who gave his sunglasses to a little girl who was helping her father and brothers in the field. She also told me stories about my father's childhood, and I more deeply understood the childhood pain he had endured.

These stories were so hard to hear, but I knew my mom needed for me to know. This was her closure. She was grieving for her life by reviewing and sharing it with me, and I was grieving with her. I said "I'm sorry that happened, Mom" many times. Those were all the words I had. I meant them with all my heart. What else could I say to the little girl who'd had such a hard life? In place of the words I didn't have, I gave my mom lots of hugs during those two years. Hugs in the morning when she got up, hugs during the day, hugs and a big kiss on the cheek before she went to bed. When I hugged my mom, I was also hugging the little girl who struggled to find her place in the world and ultimately became a ferociously protective mom to her children. She told me how much she loved me, and I told her how much I loved her. (I wish I had said that more often to my dad.)

On my last birthday with my mom, my sister brought over a cake with a candle on it. I watched my mom try to sing "Happy Birthday" to me, and I knew it was the last time she would sing to me. I thanked her for all the birthdays that she and my dad had celebrated with me, always making sure it was a special day with the presents and cake that I suspect neither of them got very often as children. I guess you could say my parents paid it forward in their own way, and I am eternally grateful to them for that.

I distinctly remember riding in a car driven by my older brother on the way to my mom's funeral. One of my greatest childhood fears was losing my mom and having to go to her funeral. Now, I was living that moment. I thought about how once, as a little boy, I was mad at her for making me clean my room, and I looked up to God and said, "Ready when you are." When I told my mom this story as an adult, she asked who God was supposed to be ready for, and I said probably her. We both laughed so hard at that. I thanked God for not listening to me, for letting me grow into adulthood, middle age, with my parents still in my life. What a gift.

When we arrived at the cemetery, I looked around at my older brother, my sister, and my younger brother. I was overcome with memories of us as children, how we supported each other, how we bickered, how my parents had taught us to watch over each other. Now we were grown adults, each of whom had found their own place in life, joining together in carrying our mom's casket to her final resting place. Four children who had achieved or would someday achieve the education my father longed for but was denied. I felt the depth of my parents' love for their children, not always expressed in a manner that would have been applauded by a child psychologist but expressed the best way they knew how.

For a moment, I stood in solidarity with the many clients who have grabbed for my tissue box and choked out the words they wished they could have one more opportunity to express to a loved one who has passed. I felt their pain. I was reminded that life is fragile, and each moment with a loved one is precious.

I gave my mom's casket a pat before I left her at the cemetery. Thanks, Mom. And thanks, Dad.

My mom's closure on her life was to share the stories she had never shared with me before, stories she needed to tell. My closure with my mom was to show her all the love that I could, starting with listening, which is one of the greatest gifts you can give to another human. And lots of hugs. My presence. That was all she wanted.

I stopped celebrating the holidays for a few years after my mom died. The memories were too painful, and I was still so raw. But I've started again. Christmas was the most joyful time of the year for my parents; my mom planned for it all year, socking away a few dollars a week to provide us with the holiday she and my father never had as kids. My parents wouldn't want me to ignore the holidays. These days, I gather with friends and we share the holiday spirit together. And each year, I try to share what I can with those who don't have the financial resources to buy Christmas gifts for their kids. Doing this, and spending time with my friends, is my joy and my parents' legacy.

I cried as I wrote this passage about the loss of my parents, but I felt a little more closure in telling you my story, taking another step in my grief process. I hope sharing my experience will help you make sense of yours.

Closing Thought: One Chapter Must End for a New One to Begin

Death is the ultimate affirmation of how life is out of our control. When we lose someone, the pain can feel unbearable. It's only human to want closure. And I do think we can find closure in various ways. But I don't think other people can give us closure when someone dies, not really. Comfort, but not closure.

But I also think, and hold in my heart, that we don't need closure after losing a loved one as much as we may think we do. Closure can help to set our minds at rest, to help us feel supported, but it does not take away the pain of loss, as much as we may wish it would. In my experience, the way to cope with this pain is to learn to sit with it, to walk with it, and be thankful that we are in touch with the tender spot at the core of our humanity that lets us feel the pain of loss. To fearlessly give up the battle to make it go away because it's not going away. By accepting that loss and pain are part of life, we empower ourselves to be more loving, more giving, more accepting. To nurture ourselves and with full hearts to carry the legacy of our loved ones forward in our lives, and in the lives of those around us.

This is our healing. This is our closure.

Conclusion
Moving Forward

Throughout this book, we have considered closure from various perspectives—what it is, why we want it, how to get it, and what to do when we don't get it. Now I want to conclude by sharing some ideas from my work as a mental health professional that I hope will be helpful for you as you navigate closure in your own life.

Reduce the Need for Closure

You can reduce the frequency of situations that call for closure by making healthy communication a daily habit. Staying in the moment and being aware of opportunities to communicate fully can help you avoid creating the loose ends that closure seeks to tie up. Note that this does not mean you should avoid conflict, which tends to let bad feelings fester and create an even stronger need for closure down the line. Rather, it means that if you communicate well, conflict will naturally arise less often, and when it does, it will be easier to resolve. Here are the most important principles to remember.

- **Communicate with intentionality.** As I have discussed throughout previous chapters, especially chapter 8, intentionality is a key component of communicating effectively. Know what you want to achieve in your communication. Be aware of the most compassionate way to express yourself. And clarify your intention with the other person.

- **Make your home a safe space for emotions.** If you or your family members have to walk on eggshells with each other, this is not effective communication. Work with your partner to be open about feelings, to be able to share them without fear of judgment or blowups. Teach your children that it is okay to talk about feelings and not hold them in.

- **Have beginner's mind.** When you catch yourself rehearsing conversations or saying things like, "I know where this is going," you're forcing your conversation into a box, one that will begin and end as the others before it have, creating no progress. Each conversation is brand-new, so enter with an open mind, ready to express yourself, and ready to listen.

- **Identify the elephants in the room.** It's not only what we talk about but also what we don't talk about that can lead to the need for closure further down the road. Don't allow feelings like anger, fear, and helplessness to be pushed aside and ignored. You're having feelings, and so is the person you're attempting to communicate with. Why pretend otherwise?

- **Tie up everyday loose ends.** If something is on your mind, say it. Don't allow it to fester and cause resentment.

And don't let an opportunity pass to show kindness, to say thank you, to express appreciation. It's okay to backtrack if you have a small loose end that's eating away at you. Tie it up.

Own Your Power

Wanting closure can be a disempowering experience, and it's important to approach closure from a position of empowerment, as seeking closure from a position of disempowerment inevitably leads to further pain and therefore a continued desire for closure.

To me, taking ownership of your power means giving yourself the freedom to be who you are. To be true to your personal values. To accept your thoughts, perceptions, and opinions as valid. To feel how you feel. It means you have respect for yourself and expect to be treated with respect by others, while also showing others the same respect. Owning your power doesn't mean being aggressive or demanding. It means having the confidence and self-esteem to show yourself and others compassion. Ideally, taking ownership comes with responsibility, including the willingness to listen as you want to be listened to, with an open mind. Here are some tips to help you own your power.

- **Validate yourself.** Sure, we need other humans to acknowledge us in order to help us feel validated, but we also have to validate ourselves. That means giving ourselves encouragement, not giving in to the voice of self-criticism, making sure we prioritize our own needs as we take care of others, pursuing our own interests so that we can continue to grow, and taking good care of our wellness. Not validating yourself sets you up to be disempowered by seeking the approval of others.

- **Don't apologize for who you are.** Owning your power means giving yourself permission to be who you are without apology. That doesn't mean freedom to cause pain to others, but it does mean living authentically as the person you are, regardless of what other people may wish you to be. Seeking closure in an attempt to make someone accept or validate who you are is a losing proposition. You don't need anyone's permission to be yourself.

- **Let other people be who they are.** Accepting others, without attempting to change or control them, gives us all freedom. Seeking closure with the goal of changing the other person's thoughts, feelings, or behavior doesn't lead to closure; it leads only to disempowerment.

- **Speak your mind, with kindness.** Honesty is ultimately appreciated, even when it hurts at the moment. Other people suffer much more when you're not sincere with them—for example, when you allow them to assume you're okay with something, until you finally tell them you aren't on board after all. So be upfront in the moment. Let people know where you stand. You can do this with kindness and compassion rather than aggression.

Honor Others' Boundaries

We talk a lot about boundaries in mental health circles as well as in popular culture. When we respect boundaries, we allow other people to be who they are while also allowing ourselves to be who we are. Healthy boundaries let us recognize when we can help and when we have to let someone figure things out for themselves, supporting them but not enabling them. Recognizing boundaries can help you avoid attempting closure in which one or both people experience emotional manipulation and disempowerment. How can you honor others' boundaries? Here are some tips.

- **Give up the need to control.** It is only human nature to want to have control over our own lives. After all, we're hardwired to avoid uncertainty. However, in our need to have control, we all too often also attempt to control others. Seeking closure can be a means of trying to gain control over another person or your relationship, trying to resolve questions in a way that you find acceptable but the other person does not. Beware of the need to control others. Consider your intentionality around closure carefully to ensure that control does not find its way in.

- **Remember that enabling is disempowering.** Enabling the destructive behavior of another person, whether that behavior is harmful to you, to your relationship, or to them, is disempowering for both of you. It can also be a way of keeping the other person in a need state and asserting your control over them as their caregiver. Pursuing closure can be a way to enable another person, such as when you ask for their forgiveness because you're trying to "be the bigger person" about their bad behavior, when in your heart you don't feel you have done anything wrong. This may let you feel compassionate and kind, but ultimately it only enables toxic actions to continue without consequence.

- **You get to have boundaries too.** As harsh as it may sound, not everyone we encounter in life has our best interests at heart. Some people are too troubled, too caught up in their own agendas, too damaged by the world to treat others with respect and kindness. If seeking closure with a person like that is risking further damage to yourself, you have the right to set your own boundary and walk away.

Know When You Need Help

Achieving closure can be a big boost for your mental health, but as you know from reading this book (if not from your own life), getting there can be a struggle, and it often never happens. Plus, whatever situation caused the need for closure in the first place probably presents a challenge to your emotional wellness as well. Humans aren't meant to go it alone. Here are some things to keep in mind when asking for help from your support network or from mental health professionals.

- **Be self-aware.** Pay attention to your thoughts and feelings. Ask yourself the hard questions about whether your intentions for seeking closure are truly mentally healthy or whether they're arising from your own unmet needs, internal stories that you continuously repeat, or even a desire to hurt another person. Self-awareness may mean admitting to yourself how important it is to you to find closure and committing to doing what you can to find it. Self-awareness may also mean admitting to yourself, however painful this decision might be, that it is time to walk away and embrace acceptance. Self-awareness is empowering because it is key to protecting yourself and others from emotional harm.

- **Asking for help is brave.** As a mental health professional, I often hear from my clients about how hard it was to reach out for help, how it made them feel weak, or how they feared they would be judged as weak by other people. Let me tell you something that I have in the past said to myself, and that I often say to friends, family, and my own clients. Asking for help is one of the bravest things you can do. It means you're doing the right thing for yourself, even if it's scary. You don't have to go it alone. Ask for help.

- **Don't be too proud to raise your hand.** Asking for help is hard, and at the same time it's simple. It's hard because we humans don't like to admit we need help. It's simple because asking for help requires only a few words: "I need help." Don't let your pride get in the way of finding help when you need it.

A Few Closing Thoughts on Closure

As we near the end of this book, I want to leave you with a few final reminders that I hope will be meaningful for you as you consider what closure means for you in the days ahead.

- **Achieve closure every day.** When the little misunderstandings of daily life build up over time, finding closure becomes increasingly difficult. Avoiding opportunities for "little closures" can create elephants in the room that are much harder to address. Make a daily practice of communicating intentionally and achieving closure in everyday interactions. Smile and say thank you. Tell your loved ones how much they mean to you. Speak up when you feel you are being misunderstood, disrespected, or unappreciated. Tie up the loose ends before they get so tangled that they threaten to strangle your relationships.

- **It's okay to ask for closure.** A lack of closure can eat away at you, building up in your mind, causing resentment, anger, withholding behavior. Give yourself permission to ask for closure when you need it. You are benefiting yourself, but you are also benefiting your relationships. Be willing to be vulnerable, to take risks to achieve honest communication, and to do what you need to do for your own wellness and self-esteem.

- **It's okay not to ask, or to stop asking, for closure.** Be honest with yourself regarding what you can expect and not expect from other people. When you know someone well enough to know they probably won't give you the closure you need, it's okay not to ask in the first place. When your attempts at closure, big or small, are not received by the other person, give yourself permission to walk away. Walking away in situations like these is not wimping out. It is saying: "I matter. My emotional wellness matters." Doing what's right for you and for others is brave, not weak.

- **Act with compassion. Always.** If books had neon lights, this bullet point would be flashing in primary colors. Try every day to treat other people with compassion, kindness, respect, and an open mind. Compassion begins at home, in your own heart and mind. Negative intentions toward yourself get projected outward toward the world. So show yourself compassion first. Turn off the voice of self-criticism and self-judgment, and it'll be a whole lot easier to be kind toward others. It takes less energy than being unkind and confrontational, I can say that with certainty. Sometimes you'll do a good job of it; sometimes you'll fail and promise yourself to do better tomorrow. We all just have to do the best we can.

- **Listen with an open mind.** One of the greatest gifts we can give another human is to listen. As you seek closure, be willing to honor the other person by listening to what they have to say. You may learn something about your relationship that you weren't aware of. You may learn that what felt like a transgression toward you was the result of a transgression they experienced. You may find closure yields a way forward in your relationship when you were anticipating a parting of ways. You may experience unanticipated growth.

The bottom line is this: Wanting closure is an innate human desire. There are healthy and not-so-healthy ways to seek it, and there are healthy and not-so-healthy ways to walk away from it. The kinds of struggles that lead to a desire for closure don't always bring out the best behavior in us, but just because you're angry doesn't mean somebody else needs to suffer, and conversely, being a good person doesn't mean allowing yourself to be harmed by someone else's behavior. When you seek closure, do it with intentionality and compassion. When closure is impossible, walk away and embrace acceptance instead. What matters most in your quest for closure is that you treat both yourself and others with kindness and respect. Love yourself. Protect your heart.

Acknowledgments

I am incredibly grateful for so many people who stepped in to support me during the process of writing *The Power of Closure*.

First, I want to thank my four pillars of support, in order of appearance:

Kathy Sharpe, my wonderful friend, read an article on closure that I had written for my website and responded with an email: "This is a book." Kathy continued to check in on my progress and encourage me along the way.

David Forrer, my literary agent, provided invaluable guidance on crafting the table of contents and the sample chapters. I feel especially fortunate that his enthusiasm for books included enthusiasm for my book. I continue to appreciate his optimism and his advice.

Marian Lizzi, VP, editor in chief at TarcherPerigee, gave me this incredible opportunity to see my words in print with my dream publisher and also provided her expert insight, her thoughtful direction, and her kind encouragement throughout the writing process.

Lauren O'Neal, my awesome editor at TarcherPerigee, patiently guided me through the journey of turning a draft into a polished final manuscript. Her brilliant editorial skills made the editing process a joyful time. I was consistently amazed by how well she understood what I was hoping to convey and her guidance in organizing and clarifying my thoughts.

I have to thank two high school English teachers, Dale Seal and Cheryl Cox, who recognized and nurtured my love of reading and writing, and my former boss and mentor, Rich Moore, who many years ago said: "You could write a book."

I continue to have the privilege of being surrounded by numerous friends and colleagues who constantly checked in on my progress and encouraged me while I completed my book. I hope they know how much I appreciate them.

My clients have taught me so much about closure over the years. I have been greatly honored to travel the closure journey with them, learning so much about closure from sharing their experiences with them, while they in turn pushed me to clarify my thinking about closure.

Mental health professionals and armchair psychologists may have noticed shades of rational emotive behavior therapy, mindfulness, and existentialism reflected in my approach. Thank you to Albert Ellis, Pema Chödrön, and Viktor Frankl, respectively.

My brothers and sister, Dick, Bev, and Dave; my sisters-in-law, Tedi and Shelly; and their children cheered me on—these days often from afar, via phone and group text. And my other brother, Claudio, shared my excitement along with his specialty pesto penne but also, when I needed it, asked, "Shouldn't you be writing?" when yes, I needed to be writing. I also felt the presence of my good friend Cord, and my beloved parents, from the other side, bragging me up and cheering me on as they always have.

Index

About the Author

Dr. Gary McClain is an educator, psychotherapist, and relationship coach with a practice in New York City. He also works with employees in corporate settings. The focus of his practice is adults in transition—romantic and family relationships, health and caregiving, work and career, and loss and grief. Effective interpersonal communication, difficult conversations, and closure are topics that he frequently explores with his clients. He is an adjunct faculty member and conducts seminars and workshops on mental health and communication.